Old print of Crichton Church, Lothian

THE OLD PARISH CHURCHES

OF SCOTLAND

Mike Salter

ACKNOWLEDGEMENTS

The illustrations in this book are mostly the product of the author's own site surveys in 1977-89. The plans have been prepared from his field drawings and are reproduced at a scale of 1:400 except for those of large churches at a 1:600 scale on pages 8,9,51 & 77. The author also drew the sketches and maps, and took most of the photographs. From originals in the author's possesion are reproduced the several old prints and the old postcards of Benbecula, Biggar, Bowden, Dalkeith, the interior of St Giles at Edinburgh, Roslin, Smailholm, Stirling and Whitekirk. Particular thanks are due to Charles Henderson of Auchtermuchty in Fife who took the photos of Cupar, the doorway at Craig of Auchindoir, Tarbat, Temple, and three of the churches at St Andrews, and to Max Barfield who provided computer facilities, checked the text, and lent the camera with which the photographs on the cover were taken.

AUTHOR'S NOTES

In chosing what to include in this book the emphasis has been to provide useful material not easily available elsewhere, or at least not in an inexpensive portable form. The book includes many remote, very ruined, or lesser known buildings. Cathedrals and abbeys are excluded except for one or two buildings long used as parish churches. The other church books in this series go up to the 1760s i.e. just before the Industrial Revolution, but for Scotland it was felt that the union of 1707 would be a suitable date to which to work. Some additions of later date to older buildings are mentioned but hardly any furnishings, monuments or historical anecdotes later than 1707. Any comparisons with English buildings should be taken as points of academic interest being made, not a suggestion of Scottish churches being less worthy of visitation and study.

The aim has been to provide several gazetteers of roughly equal length for the mainland. The regional boundaries fixed in 1974 have been used where convenient, and ignored where less convenient. Thus Stow, since 1974 in Borders, appears under Lothian, Strathclyde is split into two sections of Argyll, Buteshire & Dunbarton for one part and Ayrshire & The Clyde Valley for the other part, and Tayside and Central are taken together. The index should help readers find particular churches.

It is suggested that visitors use the Ordnance Survey 1:50,000 scale maps to find the churches. Grid References are given in the gazetteers. Where A.M. precedes the grid reference the church is maintained by Historic Scotland as an ancient monument. A high proportion of the buildings in this book are ruins. Most lie in graveyards by public roads and can thus be easily visited but a few lie hidden away in private estates. Where in doubt ask permission and remember to close gates, keep dogs on leads and leave the monuments in the condition in which you find them.

Measurements quoted in the text and the scales on the plans are metric as the author measured the buildings in metres. Additional scales in feet and inches would have taken up too much space. For those who feel the need to make conversions 3 metres is fractionally under 10 feet. Likewise it was not possible to give a table of the different centuries represented by hatchings on each page containing plans. A table of hatchings appears on page 9 and others appear in various places. The system is consistent throughout not only this book but all the other church books in the series.

I.B.S.N. 1 871731 17 8

Copyright 1994 by Mike Salter. First published March 1994.
Folly Publications, 151 West Malvern Rd, Malvern, Worcs, WR14 4AY.
Printed by Severnside Printers, Bridge House, Upton-upon-Severn, Worcs, WR8 0HG.

Old print of St Mary's Church, South Leith, Lothian

CONTENTS

Maps & notes on other churches occur at the end of each gazetteer

INTRODUCTION

Christianity reached Scotland with St Ninian landing at Whithorn c400 and St Columba's activities at Iona at the end of the 6th century. Scattered among the remote islands on the west coast are relics of early hermitages with tiny dry-stone chapels and dwellings. The earliest mortared ecclesiastical structures remaining are the round campaniles of Irish type of c1000 at Brechin and Abernethy, and a square tower of about the same period at Restenneth Priory. The church of St Regulus at St Andrews is perhaps half a century later. There the tower formed a tiny nave housing the congregation east of which was a chancel just big enough to contain the altar and an attendant priest. Foundations of a similar church lie beneath the nave at Dunfermline Abbey. Birsay in Orkney has the lower parts of a more ambitious church of c1050 with a nave, chancel and eastern apse, and there may also have been a west tower or porch. Another Orkney church, Egilsay, with features of Irish inspiration may be late 11th or early 12th century. It has a round tower west of the nave and a small low vaulted chancel without a proper chancel arch above which was an upper room. A third early Orkney church, Orphir, had a round nave inspired by that of Holy Sepulchre at Jerusalem with a tiny vaulted apse to the east. Stone, with or without mortar is the obvious building material in the Northern and Western Isles which have always been lacking in woodland, but timber is likely to have been sometimes used for building at this period on the mainland, although it is recorded that the chapel of St Ninian at Whithorn was of stone from the beginning.

The slow and piecemeal creation of a formal parochial system in Scotland began in the 12th century, although some of the more remote areas were still not served even by chapels-of-ease until the 16th and 17th centuries. The system really got under way during the reign of David I (1124-52) who was brought up in England where the system was better established. Most churches were built by lay lords and were regarded as their private property. Frequently a feudal barony and a parish had the same bounds. Often the church lay far from any settlement of importance.

Dalmeny Church

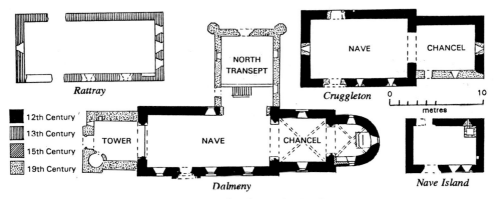

Plans of Early Medieval Scottish Churches

About fifty churches have important remains of the period 1140-1200. There are numerous single celled buildings of this period on the west coast. Most have small round headed windows on either side near the altar end at the east and a single doorway further west. Occasionally the windows are paired. Several churches lack an east window. On the mainland there are a fair number of nave-and-chancel churches around the Firth of Forth and in the Border area but they tend to be much more altered than those in the remote west. Examples are Aberdour, Duddingston, Gullane, Legerwood, Linton, Ratho, Smailholm, and Stobo. Birnie is an isolated specimen in Grampian, and Cruggleton a much rebuilt example in Galloway. Monymusk, Uphall, and Lasswade had in addition a tower west of the nave. Tyninghame, now mostly reduced to foundations, and Dalmeny, the best preserved multi-celled church of its period in Scotland, had both a west tower and an east apse. An apse survives on its own at Bunkle, and a larger example with its chancel, both profusely covered in blind arcading, at Leuchars. Fine towers of c1200 remain at Kirkliston, Markinch and Dunning. Earlier towers at Muthil and Dunblane were detached until churches were later built around them. Of parochial churches on a larger scale there remain just the west wall of a fully aisled nave at Ayr, the crossing arches and transepts at Aberdeen, and part of an arcade at Airth. Aisles in the English sense of lean-to-roofed structures extending along the whole length of the nave to provide extra space for the congregation remained very rare in medieval parochial churches of all periods in Scotland, only about twenty examples being known, most of them in towns.

After 1200 the pointed arch gradually replaced the round arch although Scottish masons tended to be slow to adopt new ideas, especially in remote areas. This can make accurate dating of buildings difficult, especially as there are few historical records relating to minor buildings. David de Bernham, Bishop of St Andrews, is known to have consecrated a number of buildings in his diocese in the 1240s, several of which, such as Arbuthnott and Burntisland, still remain. These had a separate chancel, as did Preston in Berwickshire, but other churches of this period at Cowie, Cullen, Mortlach, Barevan, Altyre, Rattray, and Kincardine (all in Grampian) were undivided single chambers, some of considerable size. Most retain lancet windows in twos and threes in their east walls but no other features of interest. Altogether there are only about twenty parochial churches and chapels containing noteworthy 13th century work in Scotland. Chapels near the castles of Skipness and Dunstaffnage are the largest and finest of buildings of this period on the west coast. There conservatism, modest size, and simplicity were the norm. Even in the late medieval period openings are often still round arched or mere slits covered with slabs for lintels. Thus, without excavation, many buildings defy being assigned by historians to a particular century.

The struggle for independance from England and the ravages of the Black Death gave little impetus to building in the period 1295-1370. Relics of this period are the large single chambers at Fearn, Lismore, and Temple, none of them originally ordinary parish churches, and the chancel at Douglas built to house family tombs. Of the last third of the 14th century are parts of an aisled nave and transepts at St Giles at Edinburgh, a tower at Inverkeithing, a single chamber with a vestry on one side at Maybole, and a crossing tower, transepts and chancel (the intended nave was never built) at St Monans. The latter two churches served colleges of priests set up to pray for the souls of deceased nobles and royalty. Such colleges were known in the 13th century but they became particularly fashionable in the 15th century. By the time of the Reformation of 1560 there were about forty of them in Scotland. Some colleges had new churches especially built for them which eventually came to be used by parishioners. Other colleges were organised from the numerous priests that attended the extra altars which by 1500 had been crammed into every nook and cranny in the large burgh churches.

The building of the splendid new chancel with aisles the same height as the main body at St Giles' church at Edinburgh in the early 15th century marks the beginning of the boom period of construction continuing until the 1540s. A splendid new fully collegiate church at Lincluden was also begun c1400. In the mid 15th century the burgh churches of Perth and Haddington were laid out with fully aisled naves and chancels divided by central towers with transepts. Stirling and Linlithgow have polygonal apsed east ends and the towers lie at the west end. Dalkeith has the same layout but the choir is unaisled. Apses also occur at Trinity College Edinburgh, Seton and Biggar, all designed as cruciform churches with central towers, although in the end only Biggar had a nave. Also cruciform with central towers were Dunglass, Whitekirk, and Crichton. It is uncertain what was the full intended plan at Bothwell, where there is a square ended chancel with a north vestry, and Midcalder which has an east apse with a vestry beyond. Rodel on Harris has a small but complete cruciform 16th century church with a lofty west tower. There are early 16th century churches with a single apsed main body with a small west tower at Castle Semple and Ladykirk. The latter also has apsidal ended transepts. Arbuthnott has a single transept on this plan. Dalserf has a unique plan for Scotland with a long fully aisled and undivided main body with a lofty tower set in the western bay of the south aisle. Undivided single chambers without towers remain at Tain, Fowlis Easter, Fowlis Wester, Innerpeffray, Covington, and Grandtully.

Haddington Church

Window from South Leith now at St Conan's, Loch Awe

St Leonard's Chapel at St Andrews   *Doorway, Tullibardine*

Construction of the larger churches usually stretched resources to the limit. Often there were several separate campaigns, parts such as transepts often being added later as at Tullibardine. At Roslin a fully aisled choir with the most sumptuous all-over decoration of the surfaces was completed along with the eastern walls of transepts upon which no further work was ever executed. Stirling lacked the intended transepts until the 20th century and many of the other churches were not finished as originally intended. Corstophine has ended up with a chancel wider and higher than the nave, to which are attached a west tower and SW transept. Muthil was a rare Scottish example of a more typically English plan with an aisled nave and unaisled chancel. The aisles engage the north and south sides of the older tower.

Late medieval Scottish parish churches are distinctively different from those in England and Wales. They lack the typically English rectilinear patterns of window tracery, their windows often being simply arched or square headed with minimal tracery or none at all. Where tracery does occur it adopts what in England would be regarded as archaic forms like the intersecting tracery at Tain, the geometrical forms in the transept at Straiton, and floral based designs at Covington, Linlithgow and Seton. Linlithgow comes closest to the English late medieval ideal with its lofty arcades, low clerestory and independently gabled side chapels rather than true transepts. Loop tracery of c1500 in windows at Dalkeith, Linlithgow, Seton, Stowe and Tullibardine has parallels in Ireland and France but not in England or Wales.

Highland churches often had thatched roofs but several Lowland churches have thick walls and heavy buttressing to support pointed barrel-vaults. Some of these vaults have purely decorative ribs as at Seton and Ladykirk; genuine rib-vaults are rare. The vaults made the churches less vulnerable to arson during raids and were covered over with large slabs rather than slates or tiles. Crow-stepped gables are a feature peculiar to Scotland. Such gables and parapets may be supported on fine mouldings. Piers are commonly round and the round arch came back into fashion. Both Haddington and Dundee have splendid processional twin round arched west doorways set under a wide semi-circular arch. The towers at Dalserf and Ayr resemble contemporary secular tower houses with gabled caphouses over the tops of the spiral stairs. St Giles' at Edinburgh has a fine crown spire. In Scotland there was no equivalent to the spate of late medieval tower building in England. Only about fifty churches had a tower before 1560, most others having a bellcote on the west gable. The collegiate churches have sedilia or seats for priests on the south side near the altar, together with a piscina. A feature found in a number of plain rectangular churches in Grampian such as Kinkell, Deskford, and Cullen is a Sacrament House or decorative cupboard to contain the consecrated host.

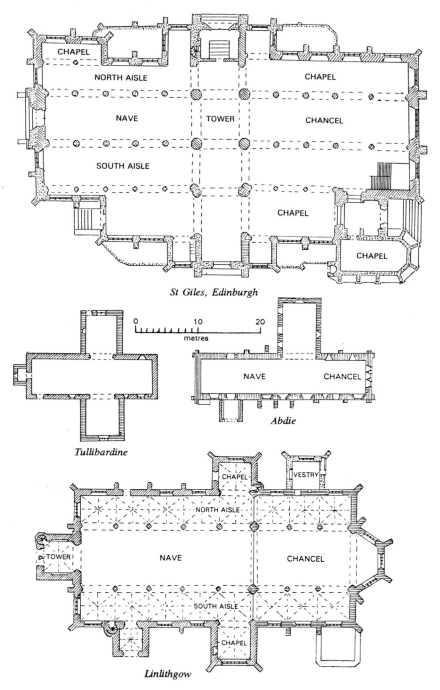

St Giles, Edinburgh

Tullibardine

Abdie

Linlithgow

Plans of Late Medieval Scottish Churches at 1:600 scale

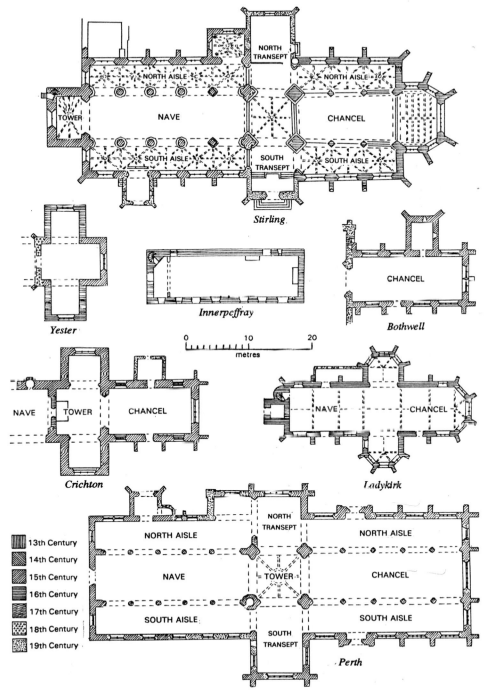

Plans of Late Medieval Scottish Churches at 1:600 scale

Muthil Church

Methven Church

From the mid-15th century it was common practice for the local lord to add a transept to church to contain memorials and a private pew. Because they continued in use as mausoleums these transepts frequently survived the destruction or rebuilding of the rest of the church as at Methven, Guthrie and Carnwath. Such transepts were known in Scotland as aisles and were much more common than the other type of aisle providing extra space for the congregation. They continued to be built long after the Reformation and enabled lairds to ignore a decree of 1581 forbidding burials within churches. In later years they were sometimes two storied with outside stairs up to a family pew set above a dark and low burial vault. Some are quite humble; others are grand, the finest being the small Z-plan tower-house added to the west end of Dalgety church.

Window at Covington

In the late medieval period there was often between the nave and chancel a screen of stone or wood upon which was mounted the rood or crucifix. All these screens and most other furnishings were ripped out by Reformers in the 1550s and 60s but even in single-celled churches their position is sometimes indicated by the window layout as sunlight was required on the screen and any altars against it. In some cases the rood was mounted on just a single plain beam. Screens might have a loft above for the use of musicians and actors. Plays were an important means of conveying Biblical stories and the Word of God in an age when services took the form of masses in Latin not readily understood by the common folk. Wall paintings of saints and biblical scenes were common but were invariably obliterated by Reformers with coats of whitewash and plaster. Medieval furnishings rarely survive in Scottish parochial churches, the majority of which are in any case now roofless. There are a number of fonts, most of them damaged and plain, although a very fine example survives at Inverkeithing, and the odd fragment of carved wood from former pews or screens. Stained glass windows were particularly vulnerable to attack by Reformers and only insignificant fragments have survived.

Cockburnspath Church

For a while after the Reformation the existing stock of churches scraped clean of altars, images and anything else that hinted at Catholicism was adequate. In addition to the parochial and collegiate churches there were cathedrals and monastic churches available for use now that bishops, monks, friars, and regular canons were abolished. The abbey churches of Dunfermline, Paisley, and Culross still remain in use, and former cathedrals at Aberdeen, Brechin, Dunblane, Dunkeld and Dornoch, are currently used for parochial purposes (these buildings lie outside the scope of this book and are not included in the gazetteers). Cathedrals, abbey churches, and other large churches were considered too lengthy for Presbyterian use. Most were either subdivided for use by more than one congregation, or partly demolished.

The first new building of note after the Reformation was that at Burntisland, a square with a central pulpit and four piers carrying a central tower originally of wood, later rebuilt in stone. The Reformers prime concern was that all the congregation could see the pulpit and clearly hear sermons. Older churches were replanned with the pulpit in the middle and galleries at each end reached by outside stairs. A central table would be set up as required for communion. Sometimes a T-plan church was created by building opposite the pulpit a wing or transept either to provide more space for the congregation as in the church of the 1650s at Ayr, or as a private pew for the laird as at Pitsligo. Either as designed from the start as at Fenwick, Durrisdeer and Lauder, or as the result of lairds adding aisles, as at Canisbay and Thurso, a cruciform plan could result. The Greyfriars kirk in Edinburgh housing a large congregation was exceptional in being fully aisled throughout its length of six bays. A dozen or so towers remain from the period 1560-1700, most of them small and plain. Bellcotes are sometimes more elaborate than before as at Kirkhill, and Dairsie has a fine octagonal corner turret. Most 17th century doorways and windows are square headed. Occasionally they are nicely moulded. Only large windows in end gables tend to have tracery, as at Thurso. Commonly there will be a pattern of two, three, or more windows between a pair of doorways on the south side. The few medieval churches still in regular use for worship have mostly been heavily restored or much altered since 1707. Sometimes only a piscina or traces of former windows revealed as a result of ruination or restoration betrays the medieval origin of churches with 17th and 18th century features. In the end many churches were abandoned and replaced by more conveniently designed buildings either in the same graveyard, or perhaps in a more convenient location for a majority of the parishioners.

Belfry, Dairsie

Burntisland New Church

As a result of the combined ravages of reformers, restorers, and ruination, the parish churches described in this book retain only about thirty pre-Reformation funerary monuments having fully three dimensional effigies. A few more remain in some of the cathedrals and monastic churches not here described. The dozens of empty tomb recesses indicate that these are only a small proportion of those existing in 1560. The majority of the effigies are 15th and 16th century knights with or without their wives, but female effigies alone remain at Lincluden and Airth, ecclesiastics at Bathgate, Fearn, and St Andrews, and a rare example of an earl in civilian dress with his wife at Dalkeith. Corstophine has a collection of three 15th century knights, and Rodil and Fordyce have respectively three and two 16th century knights. The earliest, perhaps of c1200, are the priest at Bathgate and the knight at Swinton. Late medieval military effigies in half relief remain at several churches in Argyll. Some are quite small but one at Eye in the Western Isles is life-sized. Grave slabs with crosses, parts of inscriptions, and motifs such as swords, galleys, and chalices are fairly common, and there are more in Argyll and the western Highlands than could be included in this book. There are also a few slabs where an effigy is created by incised lines. Examples are the knights at Roslin and Kinkell, and an ecclesiastic at St Andrews. The same idea was also used on sheets of brass but the three brasses now surviving in situ are of after 1560.

The collection of post-Reformation monuments is also not as large as it might be as a result of the 1581 ban on burial within churches. Only a few of these monuments such as those at Ballantrae, Kirkcudbright, and Seton have effigies as tomb chests and recesses were now often designed without them. A very fine series of about thirty monuments without effigies appear at the Greyfriars Kirk in Edinburgh (through lack of space these are not mentioned individually in the gazetteer). As a result of the Renaissance such Classical features as fluted columns and round arches now appear on tombs, recesses, and tablets. Wall tablets were very popular from the late 16th century onwards. They often have ornate frames, long inscriptions sometimes in rhyme, heraldry, and symbols of death, of rank, or relating to an occupation.

Grave slabs at Kilmory

Maclellan's Tomb, Kirkcudbright

Old print of tomb at Borthwick (showing it wrong way round)

FURTHER READING

Buildings of Scotland series, various authors, Penguin, - Lothian 1978, Edinburgh
   1984, Fife 1988, Glasgow 1990, Highlands 1992, other titles are to follow.
Royal Commission on Ancient and Historical Monuments of Scotland inventories for:
   Caithness 1911, Sutherland 1911, Wigtown. 1912, Kirkcudbright 1914,
   Berwick 1915, Dumfries 1920, East Lothian 1924, The Outer Isles 1928,
   Mid & West Lothian 1929, Fife,Kinross, Clackmannan 1933, Orkney & Shetland 1946,
   Roxburgh 1956, Selkirk 1957, Stirling 1963, Peebles 1967, Argyll 1971-92.
Scottish Medieval Churches, Stewart Cruden, John Donald (Edinburgh) 1986
Scottish Medieval Churches, Richard Fawcett, H.M.S.O. 1985.
The Architecture of Scotland, J.G.Dunbar, Batsford, 1966
The Architecture of Scottish Post-Reformation Churches, George Hay, Oxford 1957.
The Ecclesiastical Architecture of Scotland 3 vols David McGibbon & Thomas Ross,
David Douglas 1897, Facsimile reprint by James Thin 1985.
The Queens' Scotland, Nigel Tranter, Hodder & Stoughton, several volumes. 1970s

GLOSSARY OF TERMS

Apse — Semi-circular or polygonal east end of a church containing an altar.
Ashlar — Masonry of blocks with even faces and square edges.
Aumbry — A recess for storing books or vessels.
Baldacchino — A canopy supported by columns over a statue or monument.
Bolection Moulding — Moulding covering joint of two planes and overlapping each.
Caphouse — Small gabled chamber covering the top of a spiral staircase.
Cartouche — Ornately framed tablet, usually elliptical, with arms and inscription.
Chancel — The eastern part of a church used by the clergy and choir.
Chevrons — Ornament with a series of Vs forming a zig-zag.
Choir — Collegiate church chancel large enough for priests plus singers.
Commendator — One holding revenues of an abbey in trust (commendam in Latin)
Corbel Table — A series of corbels or brackets carrying a wall-plate or parapet.
Crenellation — Indents (crenels) in the top of a parapet.
Crow Steps — Squared stones forming steps on a gable. The lowest is a skewputt.
Cruciform Church — Cross-shaped church with transepts forming the arms of the cross.
Dog Tooth — A four-cornered stair placed diagonally and raised pyramidally.
Fleuron — Decorative carved shape like a flower or leaf.
Impost — A wall bracket, often moulded, to support the end of an arch.
Gothick — Imitation Gothic of the 18th century.
Harling — Or Roughcast. Plaster mixed with gravel or other coarse aggregate.
Hoodmould — A projecting moulding above an arch or lintel to throw off water.
Jamb — The side of a doorway, window, or other opening.
Jougs — Restraining irons for a prisoner (Scottish version of English stocks).
Lancet — A long narrow single-light window, usually with a pointed head.
Light — A compartment of a window.
Loop tracery — Tracery dividing a series of simple loops of globlet shapes.
Mullion — A vertical member dividing the lights of a window.
Nave — The part of a church in which the congregation sits or stands.
Norman — Architectural style (in Scotland refers to the 12th century).
Occulus — Small round window, usually placed high up in a gable.
Ogival Arch — Arch of oriental origin with both convex and concave curves.
Pilaster — Flat buttress or pier attached to a wall. Used in the Norman period.
Piscina — Basin with a drain through the wall. Used for washing mass vessels.
Plinth — The projecting base of a wall.
Quoins — Dressed (smooth faced) stones at the corners of a building.
Rere-arch — An arch over the inner side of a doorway or window embrasure.
Respond — A half-pier bonded into a wall to carry one end of an arch.
Retable — A picture or carving behind, and attached to, an altar.
Reticulated — Tracery with a net-like appearence.
Rood Screen — Screen between nave and chancel with a crucifix mounted upon it.
Sacrament House — Ornate safe cupboard for the reserved sacrament
Sacristy — Room for sacred vessels and vestments. Medieval term for vestry.
Saddleback — A plain gabled roof (i.e. without a parapet) upon a tower.
Sedilia — Seats (usually three) for priests in the south wall of a chancel.
Tolbooth — Scots term for a burgh council chamber-cum-prison-cum-tax office.
Tracery — Intersecting ribwork in the upper part of a later Gothic window.
Transom — A horizontal member dividing the lights of a window.
Venetian Window — A round headed light flanked by two straight headed lights.
Voussoir — Small wedge shaped stone used as part of an arch.

ARGYLL, BUTESHIRE, and DUNBARTON

ARDCHATTAN   NM 970353

On a crag 400m NW of the priory are ruins of a late medieval church with a lancet and two aumbries in the east wall. Ragged holes remain of the south window and doorway.

ARRAN   NS 033323

The 14th century ruin near Lamlash with a south wall rebuilt in the 17th century and a single north window marking the position of the screen is Arran's only ancient church.

BUTE   NS 035613 & 045595, NR 992705, NS 095535 & 087644

The tiny drystone chapels of St Ninian, St Blane, and Kilmichael may be of very great age. Each has a doorway set in a side wall. St Ninian's has one north window, and Kilmichael retains a west aumbry and an altar. The 12th century church of St Blane has a long narrow nave with a plinth and pilaster buttresses on the west end and north and south doorways. An arch of several orders leads to a chancel which was originally square with a priest's doorway and window on the south. In the 13th century it was extended, the new part having twin east lancets and one others in each side wall. St Mary's chapel at Rothesay was probably founded in the same period. The present ruin with tomb recesses flanked by small windows in each side wall and a three light east window seems to be a 16th century burial aisle corresponding to the former chancel.

CARDROSS   NS 350773

St Mahew's is first mentioned in David II's reign and was a chapel-of-ease to Rosneath. The short chancel with stepped gables and a fine Sacrament House in the north wall probably dates from a rebuilding by Duncan Napier prior to a reconsecration in 1467. It was walled off as a burial aisle from 1640 until the building was restored from ruin in 1955. From 1640 until 1846 the narrower and probably older nave served as a school.

Cardross Church

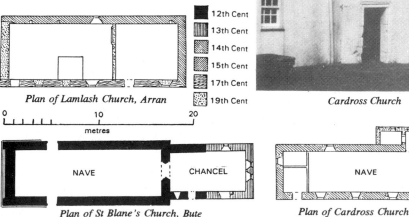

Plan of Lamlash Church, Arran

■ 12th Cent
▦ 13th Cent
▨ 14th Cent
▧ 15th Cent
▦ 17th Cent
▦ 19th Cent

0   10   20
metres

NAVE	CHANCEL

Plan of St Blane's Church, Bute

NAVE	CHANCEL

Plan of Cardross Church

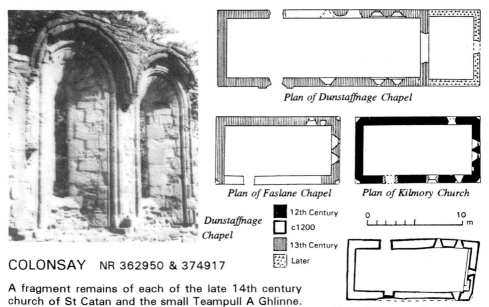

Plan of Dunstaffnage Chapel

Plan of Faslane Chapel   Plan of Kilmory Church

Dunstaffnage
Chapel

■ 12th Century
□ c1200
▨ 13th Century
▦ Later

0   10
└┴┴┴┴┴┘ m

Plan of Kilmacnaughton Church

COLONSAY   NR 362950 & 374917

A fragment remains of each of the late 14th century church of St Catan and the small Teampull A Ghlinne.

CRAIGNISH   NM 7780154

There are pairs of tomb slabs of c1500-60 on either side of the east end of a 13th century chapel with later medieval south doorway jambs. The windows are all towards the east end: two lancets in each of the east and south walls and one on the north.

DUMBARTON   NS 399755

Isabella, Duchess of Albany and Countess of Lennox founded a collegiate church of St Mary for a provost and six canons here in 1450. It had a tower with a wooden spire, a choir and north transept. The church was removed in 1858 to make way for the railway station, but the tower arch survives in Church Street.

DUNSTAFFNAGE   NM 881344

A fine chapel of some size dateable to c1225-50 lies SW of the castle. The corners and the inner jambs of the twinned lancets with round rere-arches have roll mouldings. A Campbell burial enclosure of 1740 lies beyond the somewhat reduced original east end.

EILEAN MOR   NR 666752

This chapel of c1200 on an islet south of Jura was repaired by John, Lord of the Isles c1350. The walls of the east half were thickened to carry a pointed vault still bearing the marks of the wicker mat on which it was laid. On the south side is the tomb of a priest. The roofless west half has a blocked original north doorway.

EILEAN MUNDE   NN 083591

Most of the dressed stones from this late medieval church have been robbed and the north wall is now quite low. A doorway and two windows can be traced on the south.

FASLANE NS 250898

Two windows with pointed heads cut from single blocks of stone survive in the east wall of the small chapel and there are traces of a north window and NE aumbry.

GARVELLACHS NM 640097

At Eileach an Naoimh a clay mortared 11th or 12th century church with a west doorway and east window stands at the head of a gully. West of the gully is a fragment of the north wall of the nave of a twin-celled later medieval church.

GLENBEG NR 752220

The square headed west window, two south windows and doorway may be 16th century. The masonry may be older and the more ruinous east end is an addition.

IONA NM 285241, 286244 & 287244

In the precinct of the Nunnery is the ruined former parish church of St Ronan, of c1200 but not mentioned until 1372. It has a round headed east window and restored windows near the east end of each side wall. The west end has been rebuilt. The church was given a glass roof in 1923 to protect a collection of carved stones. Close to the Abbey is the 12th century chapel of St Oran which was the burial place of the MacDonald Lords of the Isles. It has a narrow window towards the east end of each side wall, an original west doorway, a 15th century tomb recess in the south wall, and a blank east wall. Only fragments of the side walls remain of a chapel of St Mary.

ISLAY NR 311596, 458508, 344452, 204601, 285715, 291758, 335625, 114686, 314411, 224548, 390438, 164516.

The oldest church in use on Islay is the round-naved building of 1767 at Bowmore. Largest and finest of the medieval churches is that of Kildalton, of c1200. It has two pointed east windows, pairs of round headed side windows in the blocking of one of which is a grave-slab of a knight, and two doorways set out of line with draw-bar slots. The very irregularly set out chapel at Kilnaughton also has a grave-slab of a knight in the blocking of the single SE window. Here the side doorways are in line with each other and there are two northern windows and a narrow eastern one. Only the east end of the later and more thinly walled chapel at Kilchiaran stands high. It has three aumbries and a triangular-headed window. Cill Naoimh is a small 12th century chapel with round-headed east and south windows and a west doorway with a draw-bar slot. Another small chapel with twinned south windows but only an aumbry in the east wall lies on Nave Island. A chimney has been built into the NE corner. Drawings of the 1770s show St Maelrubha's church at Kilarrow with 13th century rere-arches. Only fragments now survive in a boundary wall. The small chapel of St Columba at Keills with a window near the east end of each side wall is late medieval. Only slight traces remain of St Comgan's church at Cill Chomlhan and St Columba's church at Nereabolls. The doorway of the chapel on the Isle of Texa retains a drawbar slot. A late medieval church on Orsay has been extended at the east end to create a store. See plans on p21.

JURA NR 524687 & 609822

The original parish church of Jura at Keills was replaced by the nearby church of Craighouse in 1777. Foundations remain of the small Cill Chaluim Cille near Tarbert.

KEILLS A.M. NR 691805

This small 12th century chapel has a rounded headed window and two aumbries in the east wall, twin SE windows, a single NE window and slabs in these respective corners. A further window in the south wall has a flat lintelled rere-arch. The chapel was re-roofed in 1978 to house Early Christian gravestones and a fine cross. See plan on p21.

KILBERRY NR 708641

West of the 1733 Campbell mausoleum is the SW corner of the church of St Berach burnt by the garrison of Kilberry Castle in the conflicts of the 1640s.

KILCHATTAN NM 744090

The ruined church of St Cathan at Luing remained in use until 1735. A doorway and window survive on the north and a hole in the south wall marks the rood beam site.

KILCHENZIE NR 673248

A 13th century chancel with a pointed east window, and now lacking its north wall, has been added to a 12th century nave of the same width with one round headed south window and a blocked SW doorway. The church was dedicated to St Kenneth.

KILCHOAN NM 485640

The thin side walls date from the 18th century when galleries were inserted at either end, but the thicker end walls are original 12th or 13th century work.

KILCHOUSLAND NR 751220

The cliff-top church of St Constantine was abandoned in 1617. The middle section of the north wall, with one narrow window and later burial enclosures now adjoining, is 12th century. The south wall with a SW doorway and three windows is 16th century.

KILFINAN NR 934788

The 13th century main body was rebuilt in 1759 (the date of the fine belfry) and re-fenestrated in 1881. The Lamont aisle on the north side seems to be a 1633 rebuilding of a late medieval transept with steps at the north end added in 1759.

KILLEAN NR 695445

The church of St John abandoned in 1770 has a 12th century nave and a chancel of c1220 with moulded corners and roll mouldings around the two east windows (which have dog-tooth ornamentation) and the easternmost of the side windows. The square headed SW doorway must be later. The west wall is entirely missing. There is a modern blocking wall west of the blocked priest's doorway. On the north side is the Largie family vault, perhaps 16th century. It has a pointed vault and round headed windows.

KILMORE NM 887249

The church of St Bean partly dismantled in 1876 has a round arched tomb recess on the south side, a window and blocked doorway on the west, and three blocked north windows of the 17th century when galleries were inserted. An east porch is of 1838.

KILMORY   NR 702751

The finely moulded south doorway and the adjacent window with a segmental shaped rere-arch must be later insertions to the late 12th century chapel. Original are the twin east windows and the windows at the east end of each side wall. Originally dedicated to St Mary, the church was re-roofed in 1934 to house a fine collection of grave-slabs.

KILMUN   NN 166820

All that survives of a collegiate church endowed in 1442 by Sir Duncan Campbell of Lochawe are a ruined west tower and a tomb with effigies of Duncan and his 2nd wife Margaret. The tomb lies between the new church of 1841 and the mausoleum of the Dukes of Argyll on the site of the former sacristy. The tower has three storeys connected by a spiral stair. The upper room with a fireplace had a domestic purpose.

LACHLAN   NS 010951

All that remains is the eastern MacLachlan aisle probably built shortly after that family gained the patronage of the church from James VI c1592. The doorway on the north side and single windows on the north, south, and east have all been blocked up.

LOCH AWE   NM 973110 & NN 098244

The islet of Innis Sea-Ramhach has a late medieval ruin with a north doorway and traces of west, east, and north windows lying within an embanked enclosure 28m square. The church of uncertain date (13th century stones have been found) on the islet of Innishail was abandoned c1736 and is more ruinous. A south doorway is the only feature.

LOCHGOILHEAD   NN 198014

The main body is medieval and has a tomb recess on the north side, although the doorways are 18th century, when the north aisle was added, and the windows are 19th century, the period of the session house on the south. On the east wall is a monument to Sir James Campbell, d1592, Comptroller of the Royal Household in 1584-5.

MACHRIHANISH   NR 651201

The pointed north doorway is the best feature of the 13th century church of St Kevin. Two south windows are blocked and the east wall is replaced by thin modern blocking.

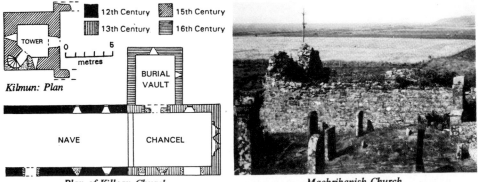

Plan of Killean Church   Machrihanish Church

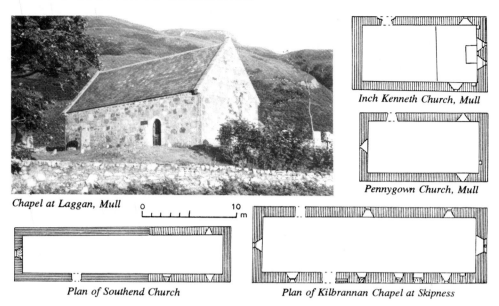

Chapel at Laggan, Mull

Inch Kenneth Church, Mull

Pennygown Church, Mull

0 ____ 10 m

Plan of Southend Church

Plan of Kilbrannan Chapel at Skipness

MULL   NM 626236, 606432, 437354, 545455, 412196, 710284, 436517, 496284.

The Caibeal Mheamhair (Chapel of Remembrance) at Laggan was given a new east wall in 1864 and was re-roofed to form a mausoleum of the Macleans of Lochbuie. The blocked windows are all of c1200. At Pennygown are remains of a 13th century church with a north doorway, side windows near the east end, and a round headed west window. Also 13th century is the chapel on Inch Kenneth with a north doorway and four windows with rere-arches formed of thin slabs. The heavy buttresses of the east corners are later. Only foundations remain of the 13th century chapel in Glen Aros and of buildings probably of later date at Kilvickeon, Killean and Kilcolmkill at Dervaig. The last was in use until 1754. At Kilfinichen burial enclosures lie on earlier footings.

SKIPNESS   NR 910575

The ruined chapel of St Brannan of c1275-1325 lies near the castle. It is a fine structure with two light windows with Y-tracery. Adjoining it are 18th century burial enclosures.

SOUTHEND   NR 673077

The eastern section of this long narrow church buried externally up to the sills of the two south windows and a single north window is 13th century. The head of a former double east lancet is reset on the low east wall. The other part, which has a round headed doorway and one window (in the west wall, now blocked) may be 16th century.

TIREE   NL 943447, NM 042472, 937401 & 984416

The chapel of Kilkenneth has a west doorway and windows near the east ends of side walls bowed inwards. The church and chapel at Kirkapoll were both dedicated to St Columba. The church may be late 14th century and has a round arched west doorway and south windows. Only footings survive of St Patrick's chapel at Ceann a Mhara, and fragments used as boundary markers alone remain of a church at Soroby.

SUMMARY LIST OF OTHER CHURCHES IN ARGYLL

CARA NR 641443 Ruin with one window and two doorways, one with draw-bar slot.
GIGHA NR 643481 Ruin with two windows of 13th century church of St Cathan.
INVERARY NN 094084 Two medieval bench ends and font bowl in Episcopal church.
KILBRIDE NM 857257 13th & 15th century fragments in church of 1706 & 1744.
KILLUNDINE NM 579498 The footings alone remain of a small chapel.
KILMODAN NR 995841 Slab of 1610 with arms & initials of Sir Duncan Campbell.
KILMORY SCARBA NM 718056 Small ruinous chapel of St Mary first mentioned c1380.
KILNEVAIR NM 889036 13th century east part with piscina. 16th century western part.
RHUDIL NR 851966 13th century chapel used as Campbell burial place in 18th century.
SANDA NR 727045 St Ninian's chapel has a piscina and twin east windows.
ST CATHERINES NN 121073 Foundations excavated 1902 of chapel founded c1450.
ST COIVINS NR 731093 Footings of chapel near Macharioch Farm on Kintyre.
ST COLUMBA NR 751767 Fragment of 13th century chapel near to a cave.
TAYNUILT NN 005309 Late medieval. South wall has a tomb recess between windows.

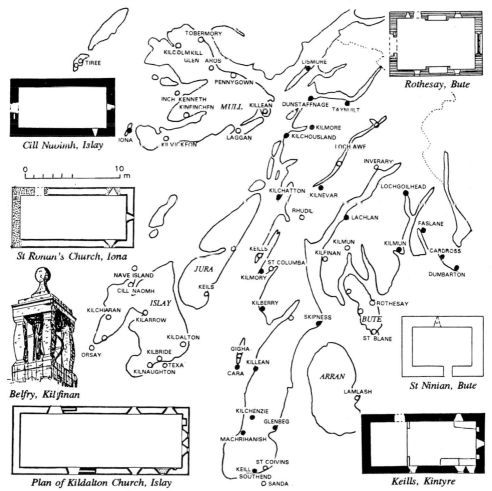

Rothesay, Bute

Cill Naoimh, Islay

St Ronan's Church, Iona

Belfry, Kilfinan

Plan of Kildalton Church, Islay

St Ninian, Bute

Keills, Kintyre

AYRSHIRE AND THE CLYDE VALLEY

ALLOWAY NS 330180

A thin later wall divides off the east part of the single body. The bell turret on the steep east gable, some of the other openings, and perhaps the twin east lancet window are of 1653, but the north doorway with an arch formed of two stones and the drain in the south wall look medieval. The church was already ruined by 1784 when Robert Burns' father William was buried here and it forms the setting of the climax of Tam o' Shanter where Tam sees through the window "Warlocks and witches in a dance". See P24.

AYR NS 334222 & 339219

The late 12th century church of St John had an aisled nave with arcades of two orders of round arches and a total width of 13m. Of it there remains only the west wall with the respond of the north arcade. The west window now looks into an ashlar faced 15th century tower at the summit of which is a corbel table supporting a parapet with roundels and a gabled caphouse over the spiral stair in the NE corner. The church lay within the outer defences of a castle built by William the Lion in 1202 but which was not restored after being dismantled c1310. In 1652 Cromwell had a large new fort built around the church which for a while then served as an armoury. The Protector donated 2,000 merks towards the building of a more conveniently arranged T-plan church on the other side of the town. This building stands complete with its original canopied pulpit and three galleries in spite of 19th century renovation, but most of St John's was subsequently destroyed along with the greater part of the fort defences.

BALLANTRAE NX 083825

All that remains of the church is a section of the south wall with a roll moulded arch leading into a burial vault containing an impressive monument to Gilbert Kennedy, 16th baron of Bargany and Ardstinchar. In 1601, at the age of 25, he was mortally wounded in a fight against the superior forces of his cousin the Earl of Cassillis near Maybole.

St John's Church, Ayr   *Chancel at Bothwell Church (see plan on page 9)*

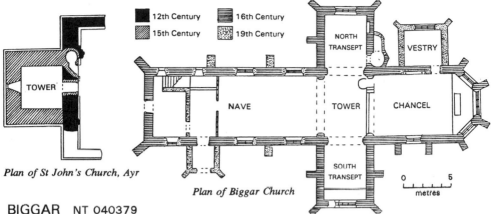

12th Century   16th Century
15th Century   19th Century

TOWER

NORTH TRANSEPT

VESTRY

NAVE

TOWER

CHANCEL

SOUTH TRANSEPT

0   5
metres

Plan of St John's Church, Ayr

Plan of Biggar Church

BIGGAR   NT 040379

The ashlar faced central tower, transepts and three bay chancel with a polygonal apse date from the period when a college was founded here by the Flemings in 1545. A string course runs round the transepts and chancel which have original buttresses, and the tower has a gunport in the middle merlon of the parapet on each side. The rubble-built nave may be older although it has a plinth and west doorway which are 16th century. It has been subdivided and has two later north buttresses. The south porch and the vestry and the monument backing onto it, and the stained glass making the interior rather dark are all Victorian. There are some incised cross-slabs in the porch. See cover.

BOTHWELL   NS 705586

The large four bay chancel with two and three light side windows divided by bold buttresses, a four light east window, a slab roof over a vault, and a north vestry, is a relic of a college founded in the 1390s by Archibald the Grim, Earl of Douglas. It contains a number of 17th and 18th century monuments. The church was dedicated to St Bride. The aisled nave with a west porch, transepts and a central tower is of 1833. Only in 1933 was an arch opened between the old and new parts of the church.

Biggar Church

Cambusnethan Church

CAMBUSNETHAN NS 806554

The belfry with fluted pilasters may date from 1672 when a north aisle was added to a main body of c1650 with many openings now blocked. The shafted archway is later.

CARNWATH NS 975465

Beside the present church is a slab roofed transept of two bays with diagonal and mid-wall buttresses. The northern bay has windows in each side wall and a doorway to the north whilst the other bay has a blocked arch towards the former nave. The transept was added after the church was made collegiate in 1425 by Thomas, 1st Lord Somerville. It contains the tomb of Hugh, Lord Somerville, d1549, and his wife Janet, and many Lockhart memorials from the late 17th century onwards.

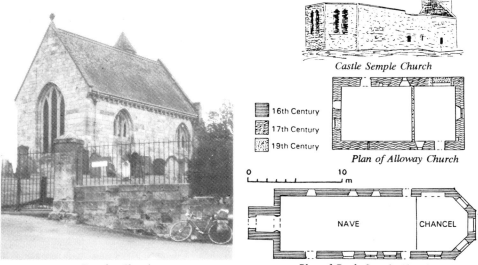

Castle Semple Church

▓ 16th Century

▨ 17th Century

▒ 19th Century

Plan of Alloway Church

0   10

       m

| NAVE | CHANCEL |

Douglas Church

Plan of Castle Semple Church

CARSTAIRS   NS 939462

In the vestibule of the church of 1794 altered in the 19th century are two 15th century carved stones. One is T-shaped and bears a crucifixion scene.

CASTLE SEMPLE   A.M.   NT 375601

This was a collegiate church founded by John, 1st Lord Semple, killed at Flodden in 1513. It has a tiny west tower and an east apse in which are windows of an unusual form now blocked. Several square headed original south windows remain intact. On the north wall is a splendid tomb recess behind which there was originally a sacristy.

COVINGTON   NS 975398

In the blocking of the original north doorway of this medieval single chamber is the date 1659 with the arms of the Lindsays of Covington Tower. On the south side are three late medieval two-light windows with various types of tracery. A transept has been added on the north side. In the churchyard is a slab to the Covenanter Donald Cargill.

COYLTON   NS 422194

The west gable may be as early as c1200 but the bell turret upon it is post-Reformation. Of the rest there remain only a fragment of the south wall with a chamfered round arch to a former transept, and a 15th century tomb recess near the east end of the north wall, now incorporated into a railed burial enclosure. An 18th century vault west of the enclosure was extended southwards after the removal of the main body north wall.

DOUGLAS   A.M.*   NT 831310

In 1307 Sir James Douglas surprised and killed the English garrison then occupying Douglas Castle whilst they were at a service in the nearby church. It was perhaps in atonement for this that Sir James, who died on crusade in 1330, built the present chancel, now the only part roofed. His cross-legged effigy lies in a recess in the north wall. An adjacent recess contains the effigy of Archibald, Earl of Douglas and Duke of Touraine, d1438, while in the south wall is a recess with the effigies of James, 7th Earl of Douglas, d1443 and his wife Beatrix Sinclair. There is also a tomb of Lady Elizabeth Douglas, Countess of Home. The church was abandoned for worship in 1780 and the aisle on the south side of the nave was mostly rebuilt in the 19th century to form a burial vault but the doorway is medieval and there is an arcade of two blocked arches. The recess in the eastern arch and adjoining stair turret date from 1565, the year given on the turret clock. In the wall closing off the chancel are two Norman capitals.

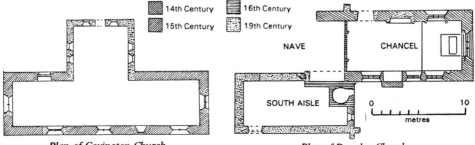

Plan of Covington Church   *Plan of Douglas Church*

EAST KILBRIDE   NS 636545

The medieval church was dedicated to St Bride. Parts of it may remain in the present building dated 1774 over the tower doorway. The tower crown is 19th century. There is an 18th century mausoleum of the Stuarts of Torrance.

FENWICK   NS 465435

This church of 1643 is planned like a Greek cross with four arms of equal length. Each contains a loft reached internally except that on the east intended for the laird, which has a forestair. Three gables are crowstepped; the fourth supports a belfry rebuilt in 1864. The furnishings were destroyed by a fire in 1930 although the jougs survive.

FULLERTON   NS 345295

The arched south doorway of the small chapel between Monkton and Troon looks 16th century. The east window is rectangular. The whole of the north wall is now missing.

GLASGOW   NS 595649

The Tron Steeple of 1637 is a relic of the collegiate church of St Mary and St Anne built in the 1480s, rebuilt in 1592, and burnt down by the local Hellfire Club in 1793. The arches under the tower were inserted in 1855. The later church is now a theatre.

GOVAN   NS 552658

On the site of the church of St Constantine is a splendid collection of Early Christian tomb-stones, crosses and a fine 10th-11th century sarcophagus.

Old print of former collegiate church at Hamilton

HAMILTON   NS 723556

An old engraving shows the vaulted choir and north transept of a late medieval collegiate church standing in ruins without a wall closing off the vanished nave. The oldest of the churches in the town was built in 1732 to a design by William Adam.

KILBURNIE   NS 314546

The main body and the saddle-back roofed west tower are late 16th or early 17th century. The ashlar-faced Glengarnock aisle of 1597 on the north with a moulded rectangular cross-windows was later incorporated into an longer aisle. It bears the date 1642 and has a loft front of c1705. On the south side is a small 17th century aisle.

KILMACOLM   NS 359700

Serving as a vestry at the SE corner of the 19th century church is the 13th century east end of the old chancel with three lancet windows in the east wall.

KIRKOSWALD   NS 240076

This long ruined church is probably medieval although it has no features earlier than the 17th century west window, belfry, and doorway. The burial vault occupying much of the interior and the regular pattern of windows and buttresses on the south side date from about the time of Robert Burns, with whom the church has connections as the real life models of Souter Johnnie and Tam o' Shanter are buried in the churchyard.

LADYKIRK   NS 406299

On a hill NW of Tarbolton is a very ruined 16th century church of St Mary with traces of two doorways and east and south windows.

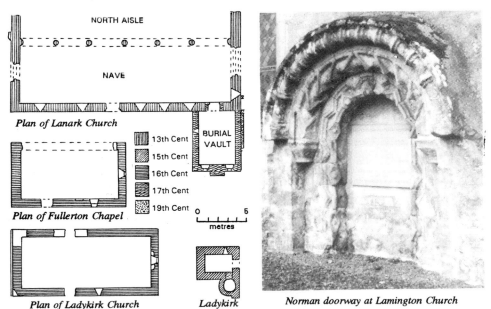

Plan of Lanark Church

▦	13th Cent
▨	15th Cent
▤	16th Cent
▩	17th Cent
▦	19th Cent

BURIAL VAULT

Plan of Fullerton Chapel

0   5
metres

Plan of Ladykirk Church   *Ladykirk*   *Norman doorway at Lamington Church*

Loudon Church

Lanark Church

Plan of Loudon Church

LADYKIRK   NS 387267

This church lay just 3km from that described above. A track crosses the site of the vanished nave. In trees on one side is the small ruined west tower, probably 15th century. At the summit are a parapet on corbels around a top stage with a short spire. On the south side are a stair turret and a single light window with a cusped head.

LAMINGTON   NS 978309

A blocked Late Norman doorway with roll moulded arches with chevrons and other motifs, and formerly with one order of shafts, survives on the north side of a church otherwise rebuilt above the foundations in 1707, and remodelled by the Victorians.

LANARK   NS 888432

St Kentigern's church was abandoned in favour of a new building in 1777. The ruined nave has several south windows and an off-centre chancel arch of the early 13th century. Of about the same period or slightly later is the north arcade of six pointed double   chamfered arches on round piers which was reconstructed in 1954. The aisle was slightly wider than the nave. The Victorians located its doorway by excavation.

LARGS   A.M.   NS 200594

The only relic of the church is the Skelmorlie Aisle, a long ashlar faced burial vault and laird's loft with interesting windows and doorways added on the north side by the Montgomeries of Skelmorlie in 1636. It contains a number of family monuments.

LOUDON   NS 493373

The eastern third of a single chamber of c1200 with two small east lancets is incorporated in a 17th century burial vault. The original west wall also survives.

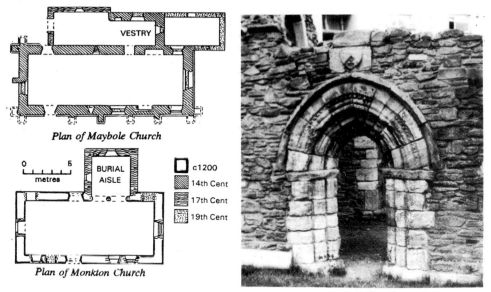

Plan of Maybole Church

0 5 metres

☐ c1200
▨ 14th Cent
▧ 17th Cent
▨ 19th Cent

VESTRY

BURIAL AISLE

Plan of Monkton Church

Maybole Church

MAYBOLE A.M. NS 300094

The church was built immediately after a college of secular canons was founded here in 1373. It is constructed of rough rubble but has features of some distinction. The south side was a show front with five bays divided by buttresses now mainly torn away. There is a shield above the doorway in the west bay which has three moulded orders with dog-tooth ornamentation on the outermost. There are remains of a pair of two-light windows, and a narrower window with a piscina in its embrasure. The three light east window with recticulated tracery and the west window are now blocked, and the tomb recesses in each side wall are empty. On the north is a sacristy to the west of which is a 17th century extension partly blocking the north door.

MONKTON NS 357277

The round arched north and south doorways date the ruined church to c1200, the south doorway having typical mouldings of that period. The north doorway outer arch, the north chapel and most of the other openings are late 17th or 18th century, although the two bay arcade to the chapel is 19th century work.

OLD DAILLY NX 226994

The voussoirs of the south doorway suggest a 14th century date for this 26m long single chamber dedicated to St Michael which is surrounded by 17th century Covenanter graves. The blocked doorway further east and four south facing windows are late 16th or 17th century. The east end was refaced with ashlar and closed off with a wall in the late 17th century to make a burial vault. A second vault now adjoins it to the north and most of the original north wall of the church has been rebuilt.

PETTINAIN NS955429

This church of 1696 was remodelled in 1820. Two of the five south windows may be original. One has a grave-slab for a lintel. Over the west porch is a massive belfry.

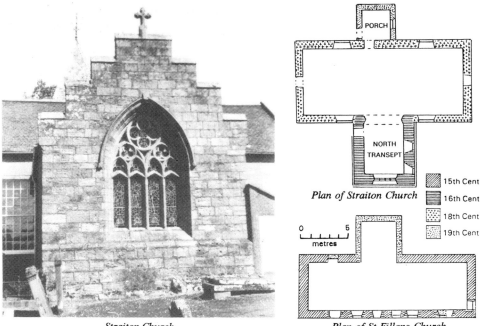

Straiton Church

Plan of Straiton Church

PORCH

NORTH
TRANSEPT

15th Cent
16th Cent
18th Cent
19th Cent

0   5
metres

Plan of St Fillans Church

RUTHERGLEN   NS 581628

All that remains of the old church of St Mary is the featureless east wall of the 13m long Norman chancel demolished in 1793. Lying in a most unusual position beyond this wall is a late 16th century tower with buttresses set back from the corners and originally finished with a slated broach spire. A church of 1900 lies on the site of the aisled 12th century nave of five bays 18.5m long by 14m wide internally. The arcade piers were circular except for the middle pair which were octagonal.

ST FILLANS   NS 384689

The ruined church may be of medieval origin but the openings in the south wall are all of 1635, the year that is carved over the doorway.

SORN   NS 551268

Most of the features of this T-plan church of 1658 date from the 1826 restoration, but the forestairs of the lofts in the aisle and each of the main body ends still survive.

STRAITON   NS 380050

St Cuthbert's is the only medieval parish church in the counties of Ayr and Renfrew which is still is use. The main body was rebuilt in the 18th century and has a north vestibule added in 1901, but the ashlar faced south transept with a four light window with cusped roundels and a gable above of four wide steps was built in the 16th century to accommodate a chantry founded in 1350 and has been divided into a laird's burial vault and loft. The pointed transept arch has a niche on the west respond.

WALSTON   NT 058456

The medieval church has gone, but the laird's aisle added to the south side in 1656 by Robert Baillie now forms the chancel of an 18th century church.

OTHER CHURCH REMAINS IN AYRSHIRE AND THE CLYDE VALLEY

ARDROSSAN NS 233423 Foundations probably of c1270-1300 east of the castle.
BEITH NS 350538 Church of 1810 contains older work and a wooden panel of 1596.
COULTER NS 028343 Remnant of church founded in 1170 beside the church of 1810.
DALSERF NS 799507 Parts of building of 1655 remain in present church of 1721.
DOLPHINTON NT 101465 Small T-plan church of 1786 with probable older walling.
DUNDUFF NS 263159 Featureless lower walls of plain rectangle of unknown date.
DUNLOP NS 405495 The laird's aisle on the south side is dated 1641. The rest is later.
GLASSFORD NT 732470 Only the west wall and a fragment of north wall now remain.
HOUSTON NS 410670 Monument of Sir Patrick Houston, d1456 & Agnes Campbell.
KILMAURS NS 415408 Rebuilt 1888. 17th century burial aisle and monument remain.
NEW CUMNOCK NS 617137 Roofless T-plan of 1657. Mullioned windows in gables.
QUOTHQUAN NS 993395 Ruined 17th century church.
RENFREW NS 508678 Late medieval tomb of Sir John Ross lies in rebuilt church.
TIG NS 116838 Foundations only of nave and chancel later extended westwards.

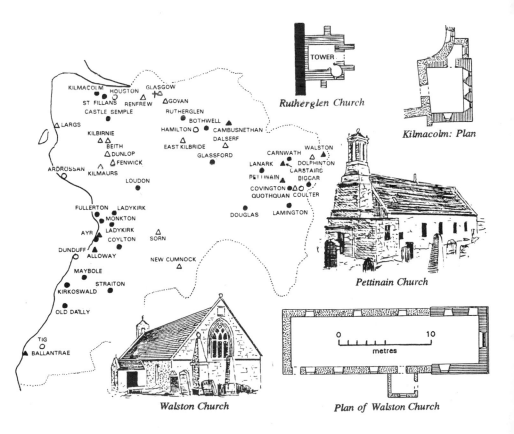

Rutherglen Church

Kilmacolm: Plan

Pettinain Church

Walston Church

Plan of Walston Church

BORDERS

AYTON   NT 928609

The very ruined main body may be 12th or 13th century in origin but the few features and the north transept are 18th century, and the burial aisle in the SE corner with windows of three round headed lights with a transom under a round arch is of c1700.

BASSENDEAN   NT 631457

This early 16th century church lacks an east window but has a two-light SE window with a piscina beside it. There is an aumbry opposite and a door further west,

BOWDEN   NT 554303

The main body has a blocked Norman north doorway and contemporary masonry in the west and north walls. The north transept dated 1661 now contains the organ. A burial aisle of 1644 now forms the chancel. The vestry and south wall are later.

BROUGHTON   NT 110368

Of the church of St Llolan there remain the east end of a single chamber of uncertain date and a small post-Reformation burial vault altered in the 1920s. A window on the south side is dated 1617 with the initials of George Haldane and Nicole Tweedie.

BUNKLE   NT 809597

Close to the later church is a Norman apse still having two small windows, two aumbries, and a moulded arch to its nave which was demolished c1820. See plan p39.

CAVERS   NT 540155

The long main body of St Cuthbert's church is partly Norman. One original window survives at the west end of the south wall. The crosswalls cutting off the west end and some of the windows date from the remodelling of 1662. On the south side is the burial aisle of the Eliotts of Stobs with an end window having 17th century Gothic tracery.

Old Postcard of Bowden Church   *Cockburnspath Church*

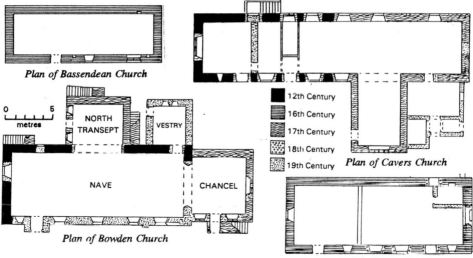

Plan of Bassendean Church

12th Century
16th Century
17th Century
18th Century
19th Century

NORTH TRANSEPT   VESTRY

NAVE   CHANCEL

Plan of Bowden Church

Plan of Cavers Church

Plan of Newlands Church

CHIRNSIDE   NT 870566

The long main body is 19th century work built on Norman foundations. The doorway on the south side of the tower is also Norman, but reset. The original tower, of uncertain date, and having a vault, was taken down in 1750.

COCKBURNSPATH   NT 774711

The long main body with diagonal corner buttresses must be late medieval. On the south side is a blocked doorway below a window and a 19th century doorway cutting into an original window. The east end was converted into a laird's vault in the late 16th century. The distinctive small round bell turret on the west gable is 17th century and the north transept and several windows are 19th century.

COLDINGHAM   NT 904660

The blind arcaded 13th century east and north walls are relics of the choir of a priory church. The other walls are of 1662 and there was much rebuilding in 1854.

DRUMELZIER   NT 134343

A burial aisle dated 1617 with initials of James Tweedie is built into the eastern part of the church which is not obviously old except for the small lancet in the south wall. A piscina is also said to survive. The belfry is 17th or 18th century.

DUNS   NT 786543

Most of the Norman church was demolished in 1790, although the chancel survived in the form of a burial aisle until it too was removed in 1874.

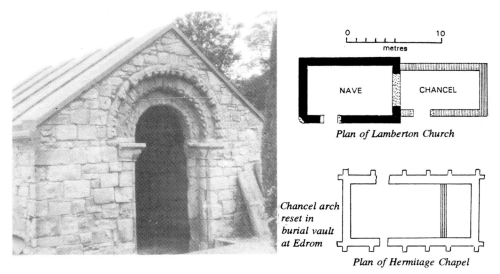

Plan of Lamberton Church

Chancel arch
reset in
burial vault
at Edrom

Plan of Hermitage Chapel

EDROM   NT 828558

Thor Longos founded a church here c1105 but the fine Norman chancel arch with one order of shafts and arches with chevron and crenellation motifs now reset in a burial vault is at least half a century later. The south transept of the present church retains a pointed medieval arch and has on one of its diagonal buttresses an inscription recording repairs by Sir John Home of Blackadder in 1696. The main body must be somewhat earlier and the north aisle is late 18th century work remodelled in 1886.

GREENLAW   NT 712461

In 1675 the medieval church was replaced by the present building. A tower was built in 1696 and in 1712 the main body was extended to meet the tower and a court house built on the other side. This was removed in 1830. A north aisle was added in 1855.

HERMITAGE   A.M. NY 493960

The lower parts of a 13th or 14th century chapel with several buttresses and two doorways have been exposed to the west of the castle.

HOWNAM   NY 777192

This church, originally cruciform, was rebuilt shorter in 1752. Most of the features are of 1844 but there survives a round headed late medieval doorway.

LADYKIRK   NT 889477

This collegiate church built at the expense of James IV in 1500-4 is the finest and most complete building of its type in the Borders. It was called the Kirk of Steill until 1550, the parish being called Upsettingtown. The church consists of a wide main body of six bays with apsidal transepts opening off the fourth bay and a similar apse at the east end. There is Y-tracery, partly renewed, in the two and three light windows. The pointed barrel vault has ribs marking off the bays. The west end has a small tower with a round NE stair turret and a top stage added by William Adam in 1743. See plan on p9.

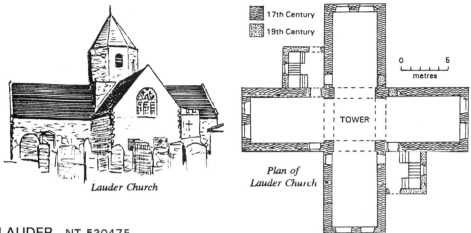

17th Century

19th Century

Lauder Church

Plan of
Lauder Church

0 5
metres

TOWER

LAUDER NT 530475

This cruciform church with arms of equal length
was built in the 1670s at the expense of the Earl of Lauderdale. It was designed by Sir
William Bruce, who was also then working on the Earl's nearby seat of Thirlestane
Castle. Above roof ridge level the central tower is made octagonal. It has four belfry
windows and a slated pyramidal roof with pigeon holes under the eaves. Each arm
contains a loft, although that to the east was only inserted in 1789 and this part
originally contained the communion table. In 1820 a new pulpit and pews were provided
and crenollated gothick porchs built to contain new loft stairs in the NW and SE angles.
Each gable has a pointed mullioned window over two rectangular windows.

Ladykirk Church

LEGERWOOD   NT 586433

The Norman chancel has three small original windows and a chancel arch with shafts on either side of each respond. This part was walled off as the Ker vault until 1898 and contains a monument to John Ker of Morristoun and his wife Grizell Cochrane of Ochiltree. The nave north wall is also partly Norman but the other walls and north transept are of 1707 and 1804 and the west rose-window is Victorian.

LINTON   NT 774263

Both nave and chancel may incorporate 12th century masonry in the lower parts of the walls. There was some rebuilding c1700 and the openings are now all Victorian.

LYNE   NT 191405

The south and east windows with loop and intersecting tracery and the west buttresses are of about the time of the pew dated 1644 with initials of John Hay of Yester and Marion Montgomery. The porch and other features are later; the walling may be older.

MAXTON   NT 610303

The features of St Cuthbert's (which is mentioned in the 12th century) are mostly 18th and 19th century but the north transept replacing an earlier structure partly covers a blocked arch, and the round arched south doorway may be 17th century or earlier.

MERTOUN   NT 616317

A late burial vault hidden away in vegetation is all that now remains of the original church. A more conveniently sited T-plan church of 1658 elsewhere is much rebuilt.

MOREBATTLE   NT 773250

A 12th century church of St Laurence burnt by the English in 1544 was rebuilt in 1757. Its vicar was Dean of Teviotdale, with jurisdiction also over Linton, Mow, and Yetholm.

Lyne Church

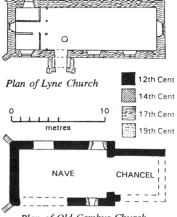

Plan of Lyne Church

▓	12th Cent
▨	14th Cent
▧	17th Cent
▒	19th Cent

0 ——————— 10
metres

Plan of Old Cambus Church

NAVE   CHANCEL

NEWLANDS NT 161465

The east and west windows and the round headed SW doorway date the single yellow sandstone chamber to the 16th century. The doorway has the date 1725 incised on the lintel and at that time the NE doorway was inserted from a former vestry, and new skews and copings were provided on the roof. Then or slightly later new windows and a SE doorway were provided. The two middle windows are more recent. The east window has been made into a loft doorway, a step having been cut in the sill. Plan p33.

OLD CAMBUS NT 804707

This very ruined 12th century church overlooking the sea has 14th century buttresses and windows. Most of the chancel east wall was demolished for its materials c1850.

PEEBLES NT 250404 & 245405

Crosskirk takes its name from an ancient cross found in 1261. It was a spacious single chamber 33m long by 8m wide with a NE sacristy. The church was dedicated to St Nicholas of Myra and was intended to house a shrine. A new church of St Andrew with a west tower, nave and separate chancel was built to serve the parish after Crosskirk was handed over to the Trinitarian Friars in 1474 and fitted out with a west tower and a cloister of which foundations remain on the north side. Both churches were burnt by the English in 1549. St Andrew's was never repaired and only the tower and part of the nave north wall remain. After the friars were dispersed c1561, the nave of Crosskirk formed the parish church until a new church of St Andrew was built in 1784. The chancel was walled off in 1656 and became a ruin. The nave south wall fell in 1811.

POLWARTH NT 750495

This church dated 1703 was built by Sir Patrick Home, later 1st Earl of Marchmont, on the site of an early church rebuilt in 1378. It is a T-plan building with a west tower and broach spire. The east end lies over a burial vault in which Sir Patrick took refuge after the failure of the Earl of Argyll's rebellion of 1684. His young daughter Grizell brought him food until he escaped to Holland. He returned after the revolution of 1688. The tower basement serves as a porch and above is a room with a fireplace reached by a straight staircase. The main body has three blocked south doorways with bolection mouldings.

Polwarth Church

PRESTON NT 787571

The 13th century chancel has twin east lancets and another lancet and a piscina on the south. The nave, also 13th century, has been converted into burial enclosures, most of the side walls having gone, but there are still three 17th century south doorways.

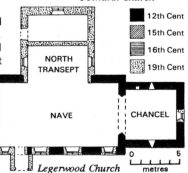

| 12th Cent |
| 15th Cent |
| 16th Cent |
| 19th Cent |

NORTH TRANSEPT

NAVE CHANCEL

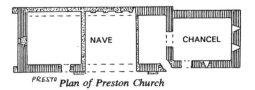

PRESTO *Plan of Preston Church*

NAVE CHANCEL

0   5

Legerwood Church   metres

Smailholm Church

ROXBURGH   NT 700306

The church itself was rebuilt in 1752. Older survivals are the monument to William Wemys, who was the minister in 1658, and the Ker burial vault dated 1612 lying at the east end.

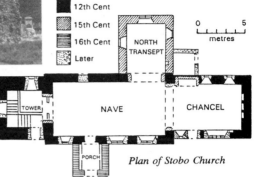

Plan of Stobo Church

SIMPRIM   NT 852454

The chancel east window containing a blocked Norman window stands high. Only low walling survives of the rest of the chancel and the wider nave.

SMAILHOLM   NT 648364

The nave and chancel both have Norman masonry and one small north window in the chancel may be original. The other openings are Georgian and the transept is Victorian.

SOUTH DEAN   NT 631091

The lower parts of a long 13th century nave with a west tower with a vaulted basement and a 15th century chancel were revealed by excavation in 1910. A new church was built at Chetwind in 1690 after the roof at South Dean collapsed in 1688. In the vault are several old stones including an ogival headed piscina and an Easter Sepulchre. A new church was built on a more convenient site in 1690.

STOBO   NT 182376

The nave and chancel of St Mungo's church are both Norman. Original are the tiny east window high up, two north windows, and the north doorway now converted to a window. The chancel SW window is 14th century. The massive base of the saddleback roofed west tower is also probably Norman, but the thinner walling above is 16th century. In the north transept or chapel of St Mary built c1460 is an incised slab with a chalice and inscription to the priest Robert Vesey, d1473. The transept vault and much of the walling is of 1928. It and the chancel were walled off after the Reformation and allowed to decay until the restoration of 1863. The vaulted south porch is 16th century and the four light south window with intersecting tracery is 17th century.

WESTRUTHER   NY 634500

The ruined church of 1649 has a symmetrical layout of doorways and windows on the south side except for one doorway being square headed and the other round. The staircases at either end once served galleries. The church has been shortened (probably in 1752) and has lost its former north aisle.

YARROW NT 358278

The church of 1640 replaced a medieval church of St Mary mentioned in 1292 by the loch of that name. It was altered and renovated in 1826, 1876, and 1906, and again after a fire in 1922. A sundial dated 1640 refers to Minister James Fischer.

OTHER CHURCH REMAINS IN THE BORDERS REGION

ABBOTSRULE NT 611127 Narrow ruined medieval body. Fine 17th century belfry.
ANCRUM NT 621248 Only foundations now remain.
ASHKIRK NT 466220 Parts of pew with initials of Gilbert Elliot & Jean Carre, m1692.
BEDRULE NT 599179 Tiny robed effigy and two fragments of hog-back tombstones.
BELFORD NT 815213 Foundations of Norman nave and chancel by Bowmont Water.
CRAILING NT 688242 Only west wall and part of north wall now survive.
CRANSHAWS NT 684617 Slightest traces in field between castle and main road.
ECKFORD NT 706270 Main body of 1685-8 and 1771. North aisle added in 1722.
ELLEM NT 727603 Foundations and fragment of south wall alone survive.
GAVINGTON NT 766522 A burial vault is the only relic of the former church.
GLENHOLM NT 102329 Only the SE corner now remains of this church.
HENDERLAND NT 231234 Foundations only of a small medieval chapel.
HOBKIRK NT 587109 Loose Norman stones in church mentioned 1220, rebuilt 1869.
KIRK YETHOLM NT 825250 Norman arch fragments and 17th century sundial at manse.
LAMBERTON NT 968574 Featureless walling. 12th century nave, 13th century chancel.
LENNEL NT 856413 West and south walls remain. Low north wall has been rebuilt.
LINDEAN NT 483308 Featureless lower walls only now survive.
OLD GALA NT 495357 Burial vault of late date lies on site of old church.
RODENO NT 230189 There are foundations of a chapel at Chapolhope.
ST ABBS NT 917687 Slight traces of chapel some way south of the lighthouse.
ST BOSWELLS NT 581315 1652, 1791 & 1826. Norman fragments. Unroofed 1952.
SWINTON NT 839476 Effigy of Sir Alan Swinton, c1200 in recess in rebuilt church.

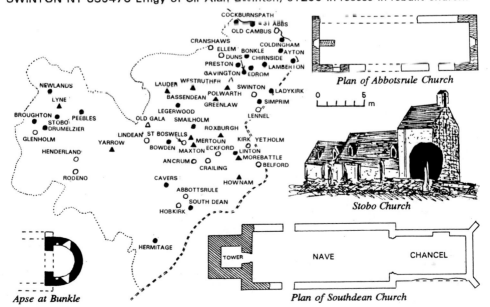

Plan of Abbotsrule Church

Stobo Church

Apse at Bunkle

Plan of Southdean Church

DUMFRIES & GALLOWAY

ANNAN NY 194665

Annan had a stone church in the 12th century as the original main seat of the Bruce family lay here. Its tower was regarded as a secondary strongpoint to the castle and was stocked with arms by Edward I in 1299. It was destroyed during the English invasion led by Lord Wharton in 1547 and the present church is 19th century.

ANWOTH NX 583552

The ruin is dated 1627 over the west doorway. The other features are of that period or later but earlier masonry may be incoporated in the building.

BUITTLE NX 808599

The 12th century nave has one original window in the leaning north wall. The west doorway may be of c1200 but the small south window and the western bellcote are 17th century. The 13th century chancel is wider than the nave and has three east lancets with a post-Reformation period doorway inserted below the middle one. The arch to the nave is slightly pointed and each side wall contains a doorway and a lancet with a shouldered rere-arch. See the lower picture on the back cover.

CRUGGLETON NX 478428

Although much rebuilt by the Marquess of Bute in the late 19th century this building retains the appearence of a small Norman nave and chancel church. Original are two of the nave south windows and the 2.3m wide chancel arch with two orders of shafts.

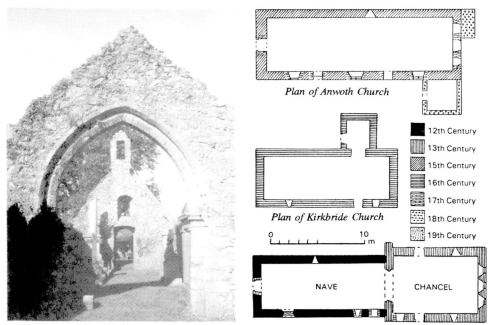

Plan of Anwoth Church

12th Century
13th Century
15th Century
16th Century
17th Century
18th Century
19th Century

Plan of Kirkbride Church

0   10
        m

NAVE   CHANCEL

Chancel arch at Buittle

Plan of Buittle Church

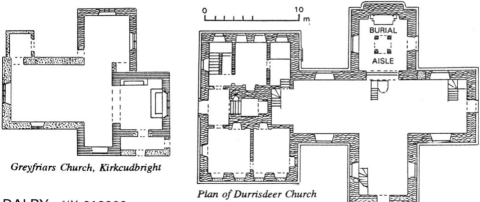

Greyfriars Church, Kirkcudbright

Plan of Durrisdeer Church

DALRY NX 618803

The burial aisle of Sir James Gordon (killed at Pinkie in 1547) and his wife Margaret Crichton remains from the medieval church of St John. It abuts a church of 1829.

DALTON NX 089747

This ruined church has a north chapel and several original windows. The thin south wall and possibly the whole structure may date from a rebuilding recorded in 1704.

DURRISDEER NS 894037

The church of 1699 is cruciform with four arms of equal length, although internally it is treated as a T-plan with the pulpit backing onto the Queensberry Aisle in the north arm. Standing over the entrance to the burial vault is a baldachino with twisted columns and in a recess in the north wall is a splendid monument in black and wife marbles to the 2nd Duke of Queensberry and his wife. The arch towards the church has a fine cartouche and a wrought-iron screen. At the west end of the church a tower rises from the middle of a two storey block once used as a school. The rooms have fireplaces ingeniously arranged to emerge in the tower parapet. The timber spire was removed c1850. Sir William Bruce is thought to have had a hand in designing this building.

GARVALD NY 041903

The remains probably date from the rebuilding of 1617. The east window once had a central mullion. The church decayed after the parish was suppressed in 1660.

GIRTHON NX 606534

The piscina in the south wall must be medieval. Otherwise the ruin is of c1625 with later alterations.

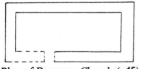

Plan of Dumgree Church (p45)

Garvald Church

HODDOM   NY 166727

In the NE corner of a graveyard near the bridge are foundations of a church probably of the late 13th or early 14th century as fragments have been found of grisaille glass of that period. Both chancel and nave have buttresses on the south side and there are stumps of the side walls of a north vestry. The nave west end is entirely destroyed.

ISLE OF WHITHORN   NX 480363

On a headland by the little harbour is a small ruined 13th century chapel of St Ninian. The doorway and three windows are original. A fourth window is a later insertion.

ISLES OF FLEET   NX 574494

Excavations on the site of a stone church of c800 on Larry's Isle discovered traces of an earlier timber oratory and the succeeding 13th century domestic hall.

KIRKBRIDE   NT 855056

The name suggests a dedication to St Bride or Bridget. A doorway and window in the small ruined church with a north vestry are original early 16th century work.

KIRKCONNELL   NY 250754

Hidden away in woodland is the only relic of the church, a 16th or 17th century aisle containing a laird's loft or pew above a burial vault.

KIRKCUDBRIGHT   NX 684107

The modest Greyfriars church contains no remains earlier than the Reformation, but the chancel and narrow south vestry are probably of the 1570s, and there is a tomb of 1597. The north transept is of uncertain date and the nave is Victorian. See plan p41.

KIRKDALE   NX 513540

The scanty traces suggest a long and wide 13th century single chamber. A much later burial enclosure occupies the SE corner.

KIRKINDAR   NX 970643

This is a thinly walled structure of uncertain date on an islet. The western part has been converted into a dwelling, now itself a ruin.

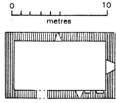

Chapel at Isle of Whithorn

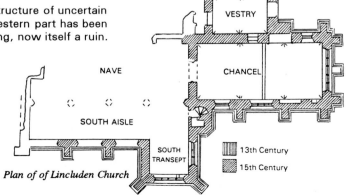

Plan of of Lincluden Church

Old print of Lincluden Church

KIRKLAND   NX 810903

The two end walls remain of a church of c1200 about 30m long. The east gable contains two round headed lancets and the west wall has a blocked doorway.

KIRKMAIDEN   NX 363400

The chancel has been converted into a burial vault. The blocked chancel arch is 13th century. The south doorway of the shortened nave could be 12th century work.

LINCLUDEN   A.M.   NX 967779

This collegiate church was founded c1400 by Archibald the Grim, Earl of Douglas. He died that year and the church is probably mostly of the time of his son whose widow, Margaret, sister of James I, d1440, has a very fine monument and effigy on the north side of the ruined chancel. This part has two and three light side windows, a set of sedilia, and an east window once divided into five lights. Little remains of the rib vault. A comparatively narrow arch connects the chancel with a much more ruinous nave which had a four bay arcade to a south aisle and south transept. North of the chancel is a range of buildings forming part of the accommodation for the Provost and twelve canons. There are six vaulted cellars entered from the west. The stair turret was added in the 1560s when Provost Stewart adapted the range as a private fortified house.

MINNIGAFF   NX 410666

The features of this ruin beside a motte on a promontory appear all 17th and 18th century although the masonry may be older and there is a twin lancet window of uncertain date set above a roll-moulded doorway in the east wall. See photo page 44.

MOFFAT   NT 074055 & 086054

By a farm west of the town are the end gables of a late 13th century chapel of St Cuthbert. The east window was of three simply arched lights under a pointed head. Only a small fragment dated 1665 with initials of Andrew Johnstone and his wife Natalie Douglas survives of a later church in the middle of the town. See plan page 44.

FIFE

ABDIE NO 260164

The ruined old church of St Magridin is essentially that which in 1242 was consecrated by David de Bernham, Bishop of St Andrews. The east wall has three lancets and in the side walls are several other lancets and a priest's doorway plus some buttresses. The more boldly projecting buttresses and the main south doorway and porch and other features are 17th century. On the north side is the large Denmylne Aisle of 1661 with a round arched opening. On the west wall is a 17th century belcote. In the aisle is a tablet to its builders, Michael Balfour and Katherine Napier, and another to Sir Michael and Sir James Barfour. Other monuments include those of Alexander Spens and Katherine Arnot, c1700, Rodrick Thomstone, d1673, and Gavin Adamson, d1690.

ABERDOUR NT 194855

St Fillan's was ruined by 1790 but restored in 1926. The chancel is mostly of 1140 and has four small restored windows. Two more can be traced in the nave. A south aisle with a three bay arcade and south porch were added c1500-10. Alterations were carried out in 1588 and the transeptal Phin aisle on the north was added on 1608.

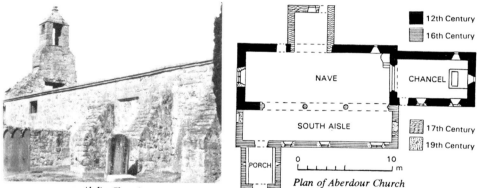

Abdie Church

Plan of Aberdour Church

Aberdour Church

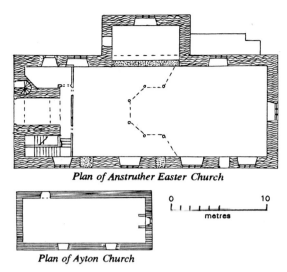

Plan of Anstruther Easter Church

0   10
metres

Plan of Ayton Church

Anstruther Wester Church

ANSTRUTHER EASTER   NO 566037

Anstruther Easter was separated from Kilrenny parish in 1640 and a new church begun in 1634 was completed by 1644. It is a T-plan with a shallow north transept (now walled off) and a plain harled west tower with a NW stair turret and a corbelled-out belfry and clock stage. The tower lies entirely within the wide main body, being flanked by a vestry and the gallery staircase. The ashlar-faced south front has three doorways, two of them now blocked. Two are dated 1634 and 1934, the latter surely a mistake.

ANSTRUTHER WESTER   NO 564036

This church by the shore now serves as a hall. A 16th century tower with pairs of rounded headed belfry windows and a slated broach spire with a balustraded parapet lies at one end of a short but wide box probably of 1846.

AUCHTERDERRAN   NO 214960

The oldest parts are now the 17th century north transept and the adjoining burial aisle of 1676 of the Kininmonths. A main body of 1789 replaces a longer medieval one.

AYTON   NO 299184

No features of interest survive in the ruined church.

BALCASKIE   NO 523034

The ruined chapel west of the house is probably late medieval despite the 13th century looking east lancet. A north doorway was constructed from fragment of old tombstones in the rebuilding of 1597-1602, and repairs were made in 1843.

BALLINGRY   NT 174977

This was a small T-plan church with a main body of 1831 and north aisle dated 1661 until a large south extension was added in 1964-6. A bell dated 1658 with the name Malcolme of Lochore lies in a reset contemporary belfry on the west gable.

BURNTISLAND   NT 233864 & 234857

The ruined medieval church of St Serf lies in desolate surroundings amidst a housing estate. It is essentially the building consecrated in 1242. Of the nave only the west gable with a lancet stands high. The sharply pointed chancel arch lies on simple imposts. The only openings in the chancel were the lancet and priest's doorway in the south wall. To the south is a tiny 13th century chapel, once vaulted and intended to house a holy relic. A 15th century aisle joining it to the nave is now mostly destroyed.

The old church was abandoned in favour of the new church begun c1590 and completed in 1600. It is 18.3m square internally with in the middle four piers supporting a steeple originally of wood but rebuilt in stone in 1748. The church is entered by a west porch and has two large windows in each side except to the north where there are three. There are boldly projecting diagonal corner buttresses from which are taken arches across to the central tower. The date stone of 1592 over the porch entrance is reset. The doorway at the head of an outside stair to the Sailors' loft is dated 1679. Inside are galleries on each side with the dates 1622 and 1733, the latter noting when they were repainted. There are box pews of 1725 and 1742 and a magistrates pew of 1606 with the arms and initials of Sir Robert Melville and Joanna Hamilton.

CARNOCK   NT 041890

The small ruined church of c1200 has two original lancets in the east wall and another in the north wall. The round arched and lintelled south windows plus the porch date from the alterations and repairs of 1602 and 1641. On the SE skewputt are the initials of Sir George Bruce who paid for the work of 1602. In the porch is what appears to be a damaged and reset medieval stoup.

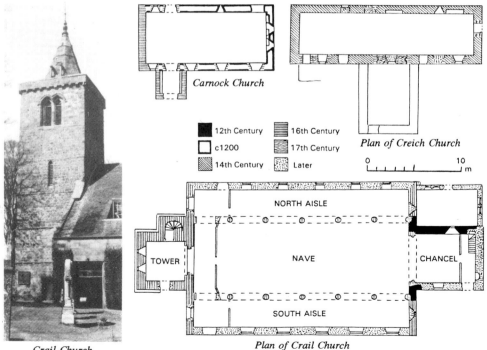

Carnock Church

■ 12th Century	▤ 16th Century
□ c1200	▦ 17th Century
▨ 14th Century	▒ Later

Plan of Creich Church

0 _____ 10 m

NORTH AISLE

TOWER   NAVE   CHANCEL

SOUTH AISLE

Plan of Crail Church

Crail Church

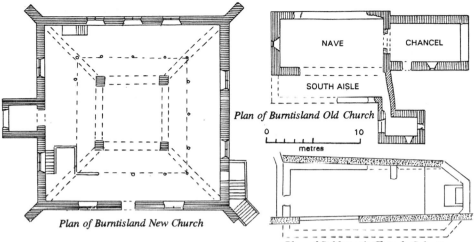

NAVE

CHANCEL

SOUTH AISLE

Plan of Burntisland Old Church

0   10

metres

Plan of Burntisland New Church

Plan of St Mungo's Chapel, Culross

CRAIL NO 614080

The eastern corners of the nave and the chancel north wall are late 12th century work. By 1243, when it was dedicated to St Maelrubba by the Bishop of St Andrews, the church had attained its present size and was then one of the largest village churches in Scotland. It is fully aisled and has arcades of six pointed arches on round piers and a west tower with twin west lancets and a stair turret on the north side. It was known as St Mary's by the 16th century when it was made collegiate and the chancel lengthened. However the chancel was later restored about to its original size and now has a 20th century vestry on the north. The upper part of the north aisle wall was rebuilt in the 1790s and in 1815 the south aisle wall was rebuilt, a medieval south porch and various burial aisles being swept away. Stones in the porch include a Celtic cross-slab with beasts and a tomb slab of Sir James Ewart, college chaplain in 1544-55.

CREICH NO 326214

The ruined church of St Devenic has a round headed east lancet and a sharply pointed south doorway, perhaps both 14th century. There are two tomb recesses in the north wall with round arches with roll and hollow mouldings. The mutilated eastern recess had a keystone with the arms of the Barclays of Pearston and once contained an incised slab of a knight and lady thought to be David Barclay, d1400, and Helen Douglas, d1421. On the south side is the lower part of an early 16th century chapel with the arch to it now blocked. The other openings are 18th century but on the rebuilt west gable is a stone with the date 1621.

CULROSS NS 990862, 988863, & 980865

Some way NW of the town is the ruined West Kirk, a medieval building abandoned in favour of the 13th century choir and transepts of the Cistercian abbey church for parochial use. No ancient openings survive and the crow-stepped burial aisle on the south and the nave doorways are 17th century. The doorway lintels are medieval grave slabs incised with swords. Other slabs have been reset in the walls including some bearing coats of arms. The Bruce arms appear on the north gable of the burial aisle.

By the roadside east of the town excavation has revealed the scanty remains of the chapel of St Mungo built by Robert Blackadder, Archbishop of Glasgow in 1500. It comprised a nave and an apsed chancel of equal width divided by a stone rood screen.

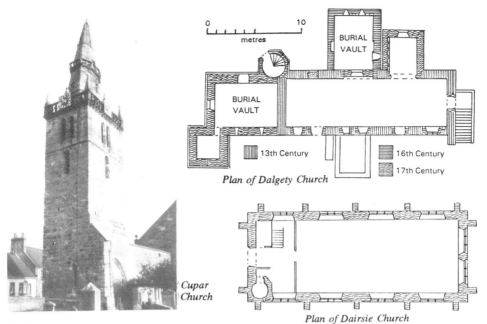

0   10

metres

BURIAL
VAULT

BURIAL
VAULT

BURIAL
VAULT

▦ 13th Century   ▬ 16th Century

▨ 17th Century

Plan of Dalgety Church

Cupar Church

Plan of Dairsie Church

CUPAR   NO 373144

The original parish church was sited far off to the NW. A new church in the town was built in 1415. It had an aisled main body over 40m long and a NW tower with the lowest two levels both vaulted. The top stage and a spire were added in 1620. By 1785 the church was very decayed and was demolished and rebuilt except for the tower and part of the north aisle converted into a session house. There are several 17th century monuments outside, including a stone to three Covenanters executed in 1680-1.

DAIRSIE   NO 414160

St Mary's church bears over the west doorway the arms of Archbishop John Spottiswode, who built it in 1621. It has a wide four bay body with buttresses between three light windows with hoodmoulds. The western bay forms a lobby and originally the east bay formed a chancel. At the SW corner is an octagonal belfry with a balustrade and stone spire. The original flat roof was replaced by a hipped slate roof in 1794.

DALGETY   A.M.*   NT 169838

The basic walling and the north doorway remain of the church of St Bridget overlooking the Firth of Forth which was consecrated in 1244. In the late 16th century galleries were inserted at either end, an outside stair for one still remaining at the east end. A new south doorway was provided and a transept called the Fordell aisle was added on the north. East of this is an early 17th century burial vault built by William Inglis of Otterston. In c1610 the Earl of Dunfermline added the ashlar faced burial vault and laird's loft at the west end. It is designed like a small Z-plan tower house with a wing containing a retiring room with a fireplace at the SW corner and a polygonal staircase turret at the NE corner. The loft once had a plaster vaulted ceiling. Among the grave slabs and memorials on and around the ruined church include those of two William Abernethys of 1540 and 1612, Janet Inglis, d1681, and Robert Meikle, c1685.

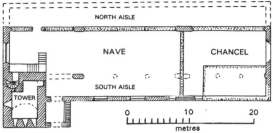

Plan of Dysart Church

DYSART   NT 303928

The remains of St Self's church near the shore are marked out from afar by the lofty fortress-like six storey tower filling the west bay of the southern body of an aisled rectangle of eight bays built c1500. It has a gabled roof set inside a plain parapet carried on corbelling with a caphouse over the stair in the NW corner. Next to the tower is a slightly later south porch. Some of the arcade piers still remain, but only those at the west still carry arches, and the north aisle has been totally destroyed.

Dysart Church

ELLIE   NO 492002

This is a T-plan church opened in 1639 and built at the expense of William Scott of Ardross. An inscription records that Sir John Anstruther paid for the tower of 1726 which turns from a square to an octagon, and then into a round arcaded belfry with a stone dome. In 1831 the south doorways were blocked and new windows provided. Inside stairs to galleries replaced outside ones in 1855, and the east porch, NE organ chamber and vestry were added in 1905. There are 17th century monuments outside.

Plan of Dalgety Church

Arcade at Kilconquhar

Tower at Inverkeithing

Font, Inverkeithing

Plan of Leuchars Church

INVERKEITHING   NT 130830

The main body of St Peter's church was rebuilt after a fire in 1825 leaving only the fine 14th century west tower and a splendid font of c1398. The tower has a polygonal stair turret at the SE corner, buttresses at the other corners, two light belfry windows, and a low 16th century parapet on corbels surrounding a lead covered spire of 1835 which replaces another put up in 1731. The font has a six sided bowl on clustered shafts. Each side has an heraldic shield held by an angel. Apart from the royal arms and those of Robert III and Annabella Drummond there are arms of the families of Stewart, Foulis of Colinton with Bruce of Balcaskie, Melville of Glenbervie, and Ramsay of Denoune.

KEMBACK   NO 419152

This ruined T-plan church was built in 1582, the year that appears on a stone over the doorway. There were transomed windows in the gables and small rectangular ones in the south wall. The asymmetrically positioned north transept is reduced to low walls and has a blocked segmental arch to the church. The west window and the eastern of the two south doorways are probably of the remodelling recorded in 1760.

KILCONQUHAR   NO 485020

The three bay late medieval arcade for a former north aisle is incorporated into a burial enclosure. The corbel at the east end may be for a rood beam. Within the enclosure is a grave slab to James Bellenden of Killconquhar, d1593. A 16th century slab incised with a skull and crossbones lies south of the new church of 1819-21 to the west.

Tower at Kirkcaldy Church   *Norman chancel and apse at Leuchars*

KIRKCALDY NT 280917

The old church in Kirk Wynd consists of a body of 1806-8 with an ashlar-faced west tower of c1500. It has a plain corbelled parapet around a small 18th century belfry.

KINGHORNE NT 272870

The present church of 1774 with alterations of 1894-5 has at the east end a south aisle dated 1609 but perhaps with older walling, and a north (or Balmuto) aisle which was rebuilt by the mason James Wilkie in 1774. Further east are slight remains of the medieval chancel, perhaps the part consecrated in 1242, and its south aisle.

LARGO NO 423034

The vaulted part of the church now forming a chancel bears a panel with the year 1623 in which it was built, and the arms and initials of Peter Black. The steeple rising from the west end of its roof was added in 1628, and the present chancel arch opening towards the nave and transepts of 1816 is of 1894 when a SE vestry was also added. The east window has a hoodmould and there are obelisks on the eastern corners.

LEUCHARS NO 455214

The nave of the hill-top 12th century church of St Athernase was lowered in 1745 and totally rebuilt wider than before in 1857-8, but the square chancel and lower apse survive. They have two tiers of blind arcading separated by a string course. The arches are carved with billets, chevrons and pearl-like motifs and intersect in the lower section on the chancel. In 1857 the arcading was restored and a parapet added to the chancel. The octagonal belfry and lantern on the apse date from c1700.

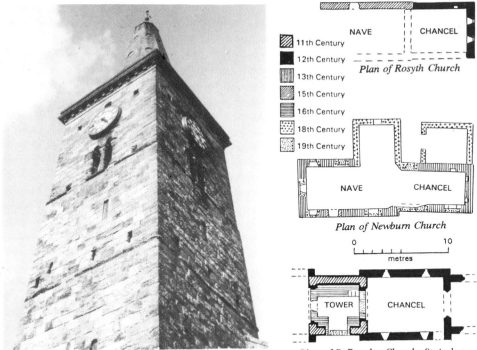

11th Century
12th Century
13th Century
15th Century
16th Century
18th Century
19th Century

NAVE   CHANCEL

Plan of Rosyth Church

NAVE   CHANCEL

Plan of Newburn Church

0   10
metres

TOWER   CHANCEL

Plan of St Regulus Church, St Andrews

Norman tower, Markinch

MARKINCH   NO 298020

The main body of St Drostan's church is of 1786 and 1806 with alterations of 1884-5, but there is a lofty ashlar-faced west tower of c1200 with two light belfry openings with cushion capitals on the central and angle shafts.

MOONZIE   NO 338177

Medieval masonry may be hidden under the harling but much of the low crow-step gabled building is of c1625 with windows of 1821, and a SW porch of 1906. On the west gable is a bird-cage type bellcote, perhaps late 17th century.

NEWBURN   NO 453036

The layout of a small nave and narrower chancel suggests a 13th century building. The piscina might be that old; the south doorway is later medieval. The north transept, the bellcote, and the blocked up windows are all 18th century.

PITTENWEEM   NO 549026

Relics of the former priory on this site are the fragment of a doorway of c1200 discovered in 1981 at the east end of the north wall and the blocked pointed arch in the south wall to an aisle which existed until the 19th century. The NW tower of 1588 with a vaulted basement served as the town tolbooth. The extension on the north side containing the stairs to the galleries and the present entrance dates from 1882.

Rosyth Church

ROSYTH   NT 085828

Of the ashlar-faced chancel of c1200 there remain the bulging north wall and the east end with two small lancets. Only part of the rubble-built north wall with a doorway survives of the 15th century nave.

Last remains of St Mary's Church, St Andrews

ST ANDREWS   NO 503168, 509167, etc

St Regulus Church

The 11th century church of St Regulus has a 33m high tower which also served as the nave, plus a small chancel which housed St Andrew's relics. In the early 12th century the church was extended to provide for the needs of a new Augustinian priory. A new nave was built to the west and a larger new chancel to the east. Both have gone, although the arch to nave survives. The tower has two-light belfry windows and a 17th century corbelled parapet. The chancel north wall bears monuments to William Preston, d1657, Anna Halyburton, d1653, and John Comrie.

The scanty remains of St Mary's church by the shore were excavated in 1860. The almost square nave may be 12th century. The long ashlar-faced and buttressed chancel and transept were added when the church became collegiate in the 13th century.

Holy Trinity is a substantial aisled church of 1798 and 1907 incorporating the lofty west tower and a few other parts of a large church built to serve the town in 1411. The tower has a plain corbelled parapet and a stone spire with a secondary spire over the stair turret. Inside is a monument to Archbishop Sharp, d1679.

St Salvator's college has a chapel of 1450-60 seven bays long with an apsed east end. The finials on the buttresses are of 1861-3 and a wooden roof of 1773 has replaced the stone vault. Within are a Sacrament House, an early 17th century pulpit, the tomb of the college founder, Bishop Kennedy, a tomb recess of c1500, and a framed incised slab to the priest Hugh Spens, d1534. The college survived the Reformation although the chapel became a Commissary Court in 1563. It was restored for worship in 1761 and became the chapel of St Andrews University in 1904.

A second chapel now belonging to the University is that of St Leonard. The side walls incorporate stones from a 12th century building rebuilt as a four bay structure in c1400, about which time it became a parish church. Two more bays and a west tower were added shortly after 1512 when the church became collegiate. When the college amalgamated with St Salvator in 1761 church was unroofed and the tower demolished. The west bay was destroyed c1837 but the rest was re-roofed in 1910 and the interior restored in 1948-52. Inside are monuments to Robert Stewart, Earl of March, d1586, Peter Brown, d1630, Robert Wilkie, d1611, William Ruglyn, d1502, Emmanuel Young, 1544, John Wynram 1582, & James Wilkie, 1590.

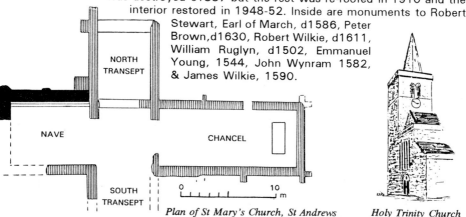

Plan of St Mary's Church, St Andrews

Holy Trinity Church

ST MONANS NO 523014

This cliff-top church was built at the expense of David II in 1362-70. The rib-vault with heraldic bosses over the choir, and perhaps also the choir windows with rectilinear and curvilinear tracery, date from after James III gave the church to the Dominicans in 1471. There are three sedilia with ogival arches and matching piscina and aumbry. In 1647 the choir was closed off from the transepts and fitted out as a parish church. The transepts were only restored from ruin and taken back into the church in 1826-8. They were then vaulted but they now have wooden ceilings of 1955. The wall closing off the tower from the intended but soon abandoned nave is partly filled with a round staircase turret. The short spire is surrounded by a corbelled parapet which was rebuilt in 1899.

TULLIALLAN NS 933881

This is a T-plan ruin with the date 1675 on the doorway into the west tower. Typical of the period are the rusticated quoins, the channelled pilasters either side of the doorway, and the intersecting window tracery with transoms.

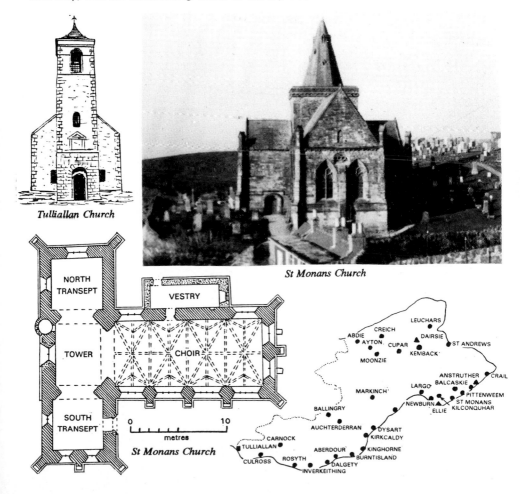

Tulliallan Church

St Monans Church

St Monans Church

GRAMPIAN

ABERDEEN   NJ 931064

St Nicholas' was the longest medieval parish church in Scotland, extending to 75m. Of it there remain the 12th century piers of the crossing tower and the much refaced and rebuilt transepts of sandstone rubble with Norman windows. The south transept has been lengthened, probably in the late medieval period, and is entirely of 1836-8 externally. It contains a brass inscription to Alexander Irvine of Drum, d1457, and his wife Elizabeth de Keith. The north transept has a large blocked arch of c1190-1210 to the former north chapel. After the Reformation the transepts served as vestibles to separate churches in the old nave and chancel. The latter was rebuilt in 1834 and again in 1874 after a fire caused the wooden belfry of 1513 to fall on it. Below the chancel is the rib-vaulted chapel of St Mary in which was buried Sir John Gordon of Corrichie, executed in 1561. James Gibbs designed the new western church of 1751-5 which is 5m shorter than the medieval nave it replaced. This part contains monuments to Provost Robert Davidson, killed defending the city at Harlaw in 1411, Provost Menzies, d1641, Marjory Lidel, wife of Gilbert Menzies, c1450-65, Provost John Colliston, c1430-50, his wife Margaret Setoun, and a big brass plate engraved in Antwerp at the expense of the town council to commemorate the noted 17th century scholar Dr Duncan Liddel.

ABERDOUR   NJ 884645

The eastern part of this 16th century church serves now as burial enclosures of the Leslies of Coburty and the Bairds of Auchmeddan. In one of them is an original tomb recess. A long laird's aisle on the south side has a blocked round arched doorway.

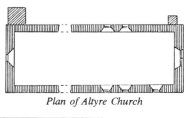
Plan of Altyre Church

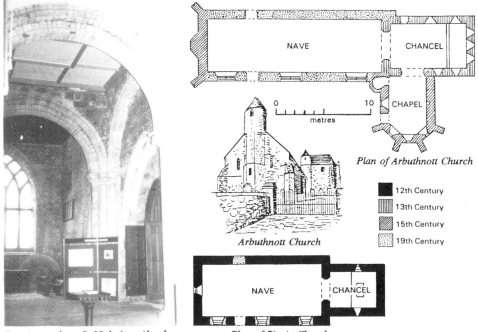

NAVE   CHANCEL

0 ___ 10
metres

CHAPEL

Plan of Arbuthnott Church

■ 12th Century
▥ 13th Century
▨ 15th Century
▦ 19th Century

Arbuthnott Church

NAVE   CHANCEL

Plan of Birnie Church

Crossing arches, St Nicholas, Aberdeen

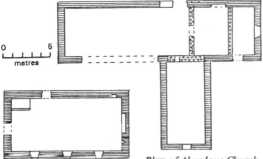

Plan of Auchenblae Church

Plan of Aberdour Church

Late Norman doorway, Craig of Auchindoir

ALTYRE NJ 036554

This 13th century ruin has a two-light east window with Y-tracery, several lancets, and a pair of doorways with round rere-arches.

ARBUTHNOTT NO 801746

The chancel with its many lancets and the chancel arch have been little altered since the consecration of 1242 by Bishop de Bernham of St Andrews. The long nave has doorways which may also be partly 13th century, although the south windows are Victorian. Projecting south from the chancel is the barrel vaulted Arbuthnot aisle of c1500 which end in an apse and has a western turret stair to an upper room. In the aisle is the 13th century military effigy of Hugh Arbuthnot.

AUCHENBLAE NO 727784

This small chapel has a north doorway, east recess, and south windows all of the early 16th century, but the piscina could be 13th century work either reset or in situ. The chapel was dedicated to St Palladius and was consecrated in 1244.

BANFF NJ 688637

All that remains of the church are a fragment of the north wall with a tomb recess and on the south side a burial aisle built in 1580 by Sir George Ogilvie of Dunlugas to contain a monument to his parents. The aisle has the outer corner cambered off, a stepped gable, and a mullioned and transomed window without tracery.

BELLIE NJ 354610

A fragment of St Ninian's church bears a monument bearing what is probably the arms of the Dunbars, not the Grahams as it sometimes claimed.

BIRNIE NJ 036554

St Brandon's is essentially a Norman nave and chancel church. The Bishopric of Moray was based here from 1107 to 1184. Original are the chancel arch, the small side windows of the chancel, and perhaps the nave doorways opposite each other. The west wall has been rebuilt at an unknown period and the nave south windows are of 1734.

Craig of Auchindoir Church

☐ c1200

▨ 17th Century

*Cowie
Church*

Plan of Craig of Auchindoir Church

BOTRIPHNE   NJ 375441

Part of the south wall survives with a round arch into a 16th or 17th century burial aisle. The arch is now blocked except for a doorway.

BRIDGE OF GAIRN   NO 353970

The 17th century church of St Kentigern is reduced to foundations except for the south side with a symmetrical rhythm of window, doorway, window, doorway, window.

CRAIG OF AUCHINDOIR   NJ 477246

Heraldic stones of 1557 and 1580 lie in the ruin of this attractively sited church of c1200 with original round headed north and south doorways, windows and a piscina. One blocked north lancet has a round rere-arch. The other openings are 17th century.

CRATHIE   NO 265947

Below the church of the 1890 used by the royal family when staying at Balmoral is the ruin of a 16th or 17th century church with a later vault at the east end. Some features remain in the south wall. Queen Victoria's servant John Brown is buried here.

COWIE   NO 884873

A chapel of St Nathalan one stood on this cliff-top site. The eastern two thirds of the present ruin, known in the 17th century as St Mary of The Storms, was built in 1276 by William Wishart, Bishop of St Andrews. It has three fine lancets in the east gable and a 16th century doorway on the south side. Otherwise not much remains of the side walls. The western part is a poorly built 15th century extension.

Cullen Church

Sacrament House, Cullen

CULLEN NJ 507664

The church of St Mary existed in 1236 and was probably then a simple rectangle 18m long. Robert Bruce endowed a chantry priest here to pray for the soul of his late Queen, Elizabeth de Burgh. In 1543 the church was made collegiate and the east end was lengthened or rebuilt and the south transept added. The south and east gable windows may be of that period, the latter having intersecting tracery. The west window may be earlier, whilst the other features and the north transept and vestry are later. In the south transept, which once contained an altar of St Anna, is a grave slab of John Duff, depicted in plate armour with the recut date 1404. The chancel contains a splendid sacrament house and an effigy of Alexander Ogilvie of Deskford, d1554.

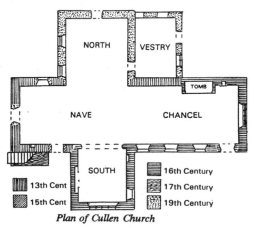

NORTH · VESTRY

TOMB

NAVE · CHANCEL

SOUTH

■ 16th Century
▨ 13th Cent
▨ 17th Century
▧ 15th Cent
▨ 19th Century

Plan of Cullen Church

DALMAIK NO 815985

The outside staircases and most of the openings in the south wall of this ruin are 17th century but the SW and west doorways with draw-bar slots must surely be medieval.

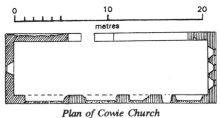

0 · · · · · · · · · 10 · · · · · · · · · 20

metres

Plan of Cowie Church

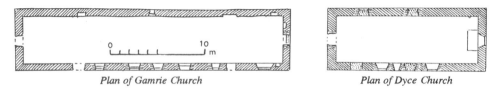

Plan of Gamrie Church   *Plan of Dyce Church*

DESKFORD   NJ 509617

The ruined medieval church of St John is famous for its Sacrement House now preserved under a sheet of glass. It is inscribed "This Pnt Loveable Vark Of Sacremet Hous Maid To Ye Honour & Lovig Of God Be An Noble Man Alexander Ogilvy Of Yat Ilk & Elizabet Gordon His Spouse The Zier Of God 1551". There are also a piscina and stoup both with ogival heads, and the jambs of a late medieval SE doorway. See p69.

DUFFUS   A.M.   NJ 173687

The main body of St Peter's church is 18th century but the vaulted basement which is all that remains of a west tower is 14th century and the rib-vaulted south porch is early 16th century. South of the porch is the base of a churchyard preaching cross.

DYCE   NJ 876155

The east window, the blocked south doorway and much of the walling of the ivy-clad ruin may be 14th century. Just the sill remains of a former Sacrament House near the NE corner. The west doorway and southern windows are 17th century. There are two Pictish symbol stones at the east end. The north wall is somewhat bowed in the middle.

FETTERESSO   NO 854857

In 1246 a church here was dedicated to St Caran. The oldest features of the present ivy-mantled ruin are two late medieval doorways set opposite each other. The north transept is 17th century. A heraldic panel dated 1602 has the Fullarton arms. The nave west doorway is dated 172-.

Duffus Church

Fordyce Church

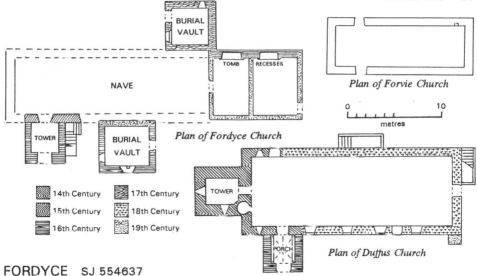

BURIAL VAULT

TOMB | RECESSES

NAVE

Plan of Forvie Church

0   10
metres

TOWER

BURIAL VAULT

Plan of Fordyce Church

TOWER

PORCH

Plan of Duffus Church

14th Century
15th Century
16th Century
17th Century
18th Century
19th Century

FORDYCE   SJ 554637

Two burial enclosures lie on the site of the chancel of St Taarican's church. They incorporate part of its north wall with tomb recesses for effigies of two James Ogilvies d1509 and 1505, and an Abercrombie of Birkenbog, c1550, the latter now being missing. A third adjacent burial enclosure built c1680 by the Abercrombies bears their arms and contains a reset late medieval doorway. A fourth enclosure is formed out of a transept which contained the chantry chapel of St Mary founded in 1516. Further west is the ruin of a 16th century two storey porch tower with the lower level barrel-vaulted. Its stair is dated 1721. In the 1680s the upper room was used as a prison. Above is a bell-cote on the south gable dated 1661. A new church was built in 1804.

FORVIE   NK 021265

This small ruin has an aumbry and two doorways opposite each other. No windows have survived, but a piscina found in 19th century excavations lies in the National Museum of Antiquities in Edinburgh. The church was supposedly founded by St Ninian.

FORGLEN   NJ 697499

The late 18th or early 19th century burial enclosure incorporates earlier material including a 16th century aumbry and a stone recording the rebuilding of the church in 1652 by George Ogilvie, Master of Banff.

GAMRIE   NJ 791645

The eastern end of the long ruined church picturesquely situated above the Moray Firth is thought to be the oldest part. The north wall is far from straight. The almost symmetrically arranged windows and doorways in the south wall are 17th century.

KILDRUMMY   NJ 473177

Only the much rebuilt north wall and the Elphinstone burial aisle of 1605 on the south side remain. The join on the north side may be evidence of a late medieval chancel being added to an earlier nave. A recess contains 15th century effigies of a knight and wife.

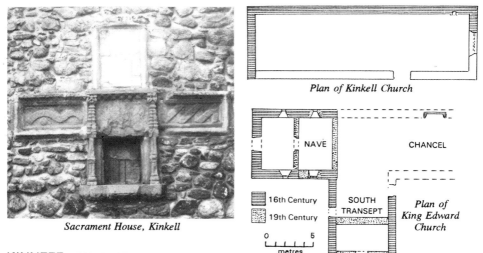

Plan of Kinkell Church

NAVE

CHANCEL

16th Century

19th Century

SOUTH
TRANSEPT

*Plan of
King Edward
Church*

0　　5
metres

Sacrament House, Kinkell

KINNEFF　NO 856749

Except perhaps for the west wall, the church consecrated in 1242 in which the Honours of Scotland were hidden from 1651 until the Restoration of Charles II in 1660, was rebuilt in 1738, and a north aisle was added in 1876. The Honours were smuggled out of nearby Dunnottar Castle whilst it was being besieged by Cromwell. They were cared for by the Reverend James Granger who dug them up and dried them out at intervals. The old church had eight buttresses and an arcade of wooden pillars carrying the roof.

KINCARDINE　NO 594994

This large 13th century church served a hospice founded by Alan Durward. Foundations east of the 18th century east wall, in which are reset two lancets, indicate a building once over 42m long internally. The surviving part has a late 13th century doorway and two original windows. Of the 18th century are the west doorway and the two windows and two doorway set symmetrically in the south wall.

KING EDWARD　NJ 709578

The western part of the nave is now divided into two burial enclosures. The west doorway is 16th century and there are small side windows perhaps as early as c1200. There are traces of a 16th century south transept now divided up inside. All that survives of the chancel is a tomb recess dated 1590 on the north side.

KINKELL　A.M.　NJ 784191

The 16th century church of St Michael's fell out of use in the mid 18th century and is now much ruined. It retains the north jamb of a large east window and near the NE corner is a fine Sacrament House dated 1524 with initials of parson Alexander Galloway. There is a slab (see p69) to Gilbert de Greenlaw, killed at Harlaw in 1411.

MARYCULTER　NO 844999

Only the lowest parts survive of a church built in 1287 by the Knights Templar, later enlarged by the Hospitallers, and later used for parochial worship until 1787.

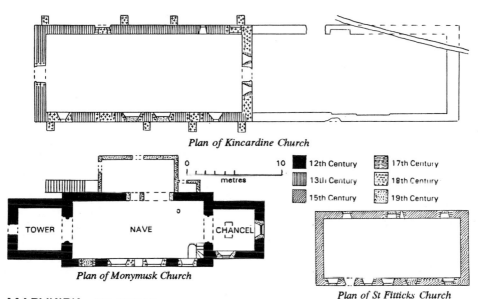

Plan of Kincardine Church

TOWER | NAVE | CHANCEL

Plan of Monymusk Church

■ 12th Century	▨ 17th Century
▥ 13th Century	▨ 18th Century
▨ 15th Century	▨ 19th Century

0 ——————— 10 metres

Plan of St Fitticks Church

MARYKIRK   NO 686656

Two burial aisles remain near the church of 1806. That on the south, containing a fine heraldic monument to the Strachan family, is dated 1615 over the doorway but contains a medieval ogival headed piscina.

MICHAELKIRK   NJ 194689

This burial chapel of the Gordon Earls of Aberdeen was built in 1703 by the widow of Sir Robert Innis on the site of the medieval church of Ogstoun. It has Y-tracery in the windows either side of a central doorway and intersecting tracery in the end window.

MIDMAR   NJ 702058

The old church was divided into burial enclosures for the estates of Midmar, Corsendae, and Kebbaty when a new church was built nearer the village in 1677.

MONYKEBBOCK   NJ 877182

In a circular walled graveyard are foundations of the chapel of St Colm. A plaque proclaims the chapel was in used from 1256 until 1609.

MONYMUSK   NJ684154

The nave, chancel arch, and parts of the west tower date from the 1170s when Gilchrist, Earl of Mar founded a priory here. The priory was burnt in 1554 as a result of negligence by the last prior John Elphinstone who was later hanged for various crimes. The present chancel dates from the 1890s and has an older burial enclosure beyond it. In 1822 the tower was reduced in height and given a spire which was removed in 1891. The doorway on the south side of the nave is of 1660, and the windows are probably 18th century. In the museum of the Society of Antiquities at Edinburgh is a bone of the 8th century St Columba long kept as a relic at Monymusk. See p66-7.

Monymusk Church

MORTLACH   NJ 324393

The sizable harled main body of St Moluag's church is at least partly of c1200-30 as it has a round headed doorway on the north and small lancets to the east. By the NE corner is a recess containing the military effigy of Alexander Leslie, d1549. The other features appear to be all of the 19th century.

OLD DEER   NJ 989477

The eastern part of the Norman nave survives as a burial enclosure and has a late medieval recess, an aumbry, and a stone with the date 1603 reset in it. To the east it has a chamfered round arch to another enclosure on the site of the chancel.

ORROCK   NJ 970197

The remains comprise the west end with 17th century features, one corner of a south transept, and a mound of earth over a burial vault on the north side.

PETERHEAD   NK 131462

Of a Norman church there survive the east end of the long nave with a plain round chancel arch and the side walls of a narrower chancel inclined to the south instead of being on the same axis. There also survives a 17th century west tower.

PITSLIGO   NJ 880562

This is a symmetrically laid out 17th century T-plan ruin with a laird's loft of the Forbes family set over a vault on the south side and a pair of large north windows opposite which lighted the pulpit. Some of the windows have pointed heads and there is a fine belfry. Galleries were reached by internal stairs projecting into the northern corners. Parts of the pulpit and laird's loft front have been transferred to the larger new church.

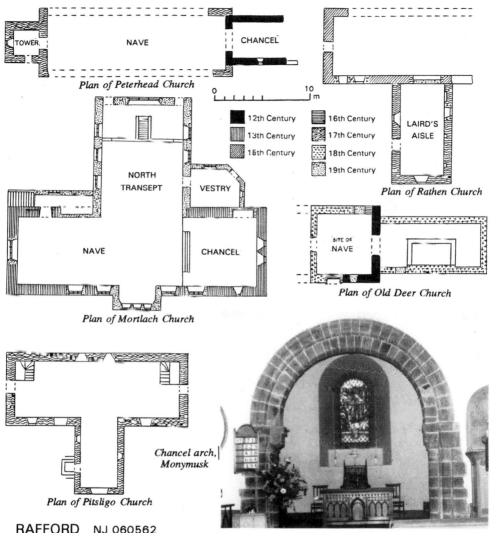

Plan of Peterhead Church

■ 12th Century	▦ 16th Century	
▥ 13th Century	▨ 17th Century	
▨ 15th Century	⬚ 18th Century	
	⬚ 19th Century	

Plan of Rathen Church

Plan of Mortlach Church

Plan of Old Deer Church

Plan of Pitsligo Church

Chancel arch, Monymusk

RAFFORD   NJ 060562

Part of the west wall is incorporated in a pair of 18th century burial enclosures whilst a fragment of the south wall is adjoined by a burial aisle dated 1640.

RATHEN   NK 001610

Only the west wall remains of the medieval church. The south wall also surviving appears to be later. From it projects a long laird's aisle or transept built in 1633.

RATHVEN   NJ 444656

The fragmentary remains of the main body appear no older than the 18th century but the burial vault on the south side is dated 1612.

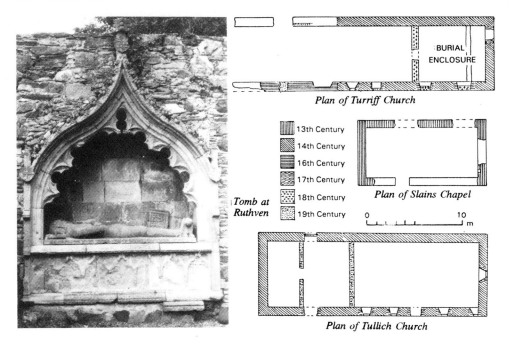

Plan of Turriff Church

	13th Century
	14th Century
	16th Century
	17th Century
	18th Century
	19th Century

Tomb at Ruthven

Plan of Slains Chapel

0   10
⌐⊥⊥⊥⊥⊥⊥⊥⊥⊥⌐ m

Plan of Tullich Church

RATTRAY   NK 085576

The features of St Mary's chapel are very damaged but all appear to be original 13th century work. They include triple eastern lancets.

RUTHVEN   NJ 506468

Only the north and west walls remain, without features except a military effigy of c1400 in a north recess and a west bellcote containing a bell dated 1643.

ST FITTICKS   NJ 963049

The windows are all 17th century but the north and south doorways of the ruin have rere-arches which suggest that the real date of the building is late medieval.

SLAINS   NK 030326

The remains of the medieval chapel of St Fidamnan show signs of having one had a large east window and a pair of north and south doorways set opposite each other.

TARVES   NJ 869312

The medieval church of St Englatius has gone leaving only the burial aisle added to it in 1589 by Sir William Forbes containing the fine monument to him and his wife.

TULLICH   NO 390975

The blocked north doorway shows that the church is basically 13th or 14th century although the two doorways and several windows in the south wall are are 17th century.

OTHER CHURCH REMAINS IN GRAMPIAN

ABERLOUR NJ 266430 West wall remains of narrow medieval church of St Drostan.
AUCHTERLESS NJ 714416 Fragments of wide 17th century church near later one.
BIRSE NO 354974 Gravestone with sword & battle-axe in porch of church of 1779.
BOHARM NJ 321465 Only the west wall with a blocked doorway now remains.
BROADSEAT NJ 709210 Foundations only of tiny medieval chapel.
CAIRNIE NJ 487410 Foundations and part of west wall remain of St Peter's church.
CRIMOND NJ 053576 Part of the south wall survives with two windows and door jamb.
FETTERANGUS NJ 981505 Ivy-grown fragment of church on site of stone circle.
FINTRAY NJ 872156 Sacrement House in NE corner of otherwise much rebuilt ruin.
GLENBERVIE NO 766807 Featureless east end now forms a Douglas burial enclosure.
INSCH NJ 631282 Medieval west wall with 17th century doorway the only relic.
INVERBERVIE NO 830727 Only the medieval west wall remains with later doorway.
INVERBOYNDIE NJ 666644 16th century west wall and burial vault on north survive.
KEIG NJ 620188 17th century ruin on site of St Diaconianus' church mentioned 1202.
KENNETHMONT NJ 539295 Lower parts of east and north walls lie in burial enclosures.
KIRKSTYLE NJ 299014 Ruin of uncertain date on slope near later church.
LEOCHEL CUSHNIE ST 506108 Featureless ivygrown remains of uncertain date.
LOGIE DURNO SJ 104264 Ivy-covered heaps of rubble mark out extent of old church.
LONGSIDE SJ 040473 Ivy-covered existing ruin appears to be entirely of 1620.
NEWBURGH SJ 004256 Only a 17th century burial enclosure now remains.
SEGGAT NJ 141504 Only a fragment now remains of the chapel.
ST CYRUS NO 747649 Burial vault with 17th cent doorway may represent the chancel.
STRATHDON NJ 355127 17th century pew panels lie in the church rebuilt in 1853.
STRICHEN NJ 947547 Vault and loft of 1620 with adjoining fragments of south wall.
TURRIFF NJ 729497 Plan (p68) indicates medieval origin. The features are all later.

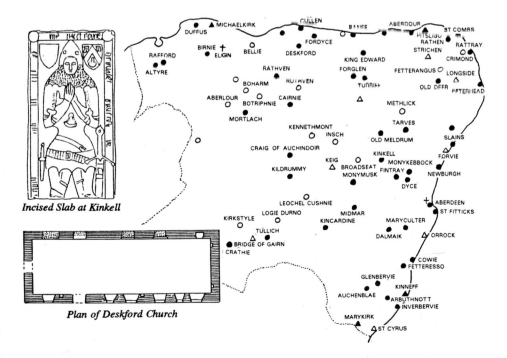

Incised Slab at Kinkell

Plan of Deskford Church

HIGHLAND DISTRICT

ARISAIG NM 659869

The ruined St Maelrubha's church containing 15th century grave slabs and other memorials is said to have been built by John Moydartach, Captain of Clanranald, d1574. It has slit windows, a south doorway, and a small chapel, evidently earlier, to the west.

ALLANGRANGE NH 625515

The eastern part of a 13th century church survives with three lancets and an aumbry in the east wall and a pair of lancets in the south wall.

ALNESS NH 644691

This church dated 1625 on the birdcage bellcote was unroofed in 1970. There is a symmetrical layout of doorways and window on the south side. The date 1775 on the SW skewputt refers to major alterations. It was perhaps then that a mausoleum originally dated 1672 (the stone has been reset on the south side) was connected to the church by an aisle. A loft and vault dated 1671 with the Munro arms lies at to the east.

ARDCLACH NH 955450

The T-plan church lying in a deep valley beside the Findhorn is of 1765 and 1836. The famous bell tower lies above the valley where its bell could be heard better. It has a vaulted basement and a room above with shot-holes and a fireplace over which is the monogram of Master George Balfour, minister here in 1655, the date on the west gable.

ARDNAMURCHAN NM 485640

Parts of a 12th or 13th century church of St Congan at Kilchoan were incorporated in the present roofless building of 1762 to the same dimensions but containing galleries.

Barevan Church

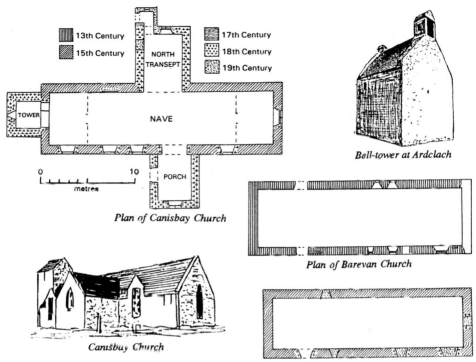

13th Century
15th Century
NORTH TRANSEPT
17th Century
18th Century
19th Century

TOWER

NAVE

0   10
metres

PORCH

Plan of Canisbay Church

Bell-tower at Ardclach

Plan of Barevan Church

Canisbay Church

Plan of Bower Church

AULDEARN   NH 919556

The church was rebuilt in 1754 and remodelled in 1898 but there are 17th century tablets to John Inglis and Janet Burnet, and James Sutherland of Kinsteary. Other monuments lie in the ruined 16th century chancel of the old church to the east. The east window has Y-tracery. The south wall was probably rebuilt c1600.

BAREVAN   NH 837473

The church of St Aibind built in the early 13th century has been a ruin since the more conveniently sited Cawdor Church was built in 1619. Original surviving features include two lancets on each side and a double piscina and two doorways on the south side. One window has Y-tracery. The end walls are destroyed. Graveslabs form the floor.

BOWER   ND 2446176

The walls may be medieval in their lowest parts but the oldest features are of the 1718 rebuilding. The west gable was rebuilt in 1803. A new church was built in 1847.

CANISBAY   ND 344729

The long main body with a SW doorway blocked and hidden under harling in 1891 represents the much rebuilt 15th century church of St Drostan. The west tower was added in 1704. The south transept, converted to a porch in 1891, is dated 1724, and the north transept was built in 1736, whilst the year 1720 appears on a nave skewputt.

CAWDOR NH 844499

A T-plan church with the south transept gable carried up as a small tower and a flat roofed porch in the SE angle was mostly rebuilt in 1829 when a north transept was added. The belfry within the tower parapet may be 18th century.

CILLE CHOIRILL NN 307813

The chapel of St Cyril high up above Roy Bridge was restored from ruin as a Roman Catholic chapel in 1933. The round arched SE window may be 13th century.

CILLE MUIRE NH 523773

This roofless but fairly complete remotely sited chapel retains small windows and a doorway now minus its arch all on the south side. It may be 13th or 15th century.

CONTIN NH 456557

The original church of St Maelrubha was burnt by the Macdonalds in the 1480s. Parts of a new church then built survive in the building of the 1730s which was slated in place of the original heather thatch in 1760, and heightened in 1832. Underneath the gallery stair there survives a Sacrament House of c1490, and there are signs of a round arched tomb recess. In the vestibule are two late medieval graveslabs.

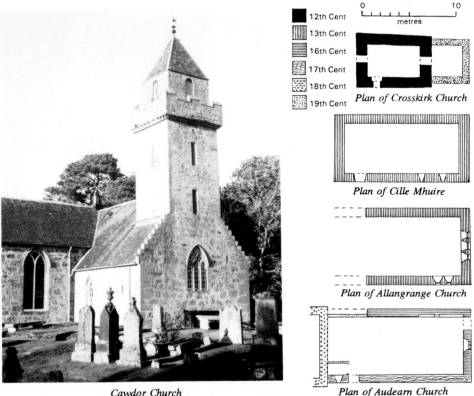

12th Cent
13th Cent
16th Cent
17th Cent
18th Cent
19th Cent

0   10
metres

Plan of Crosskirk Church

Plan of Cille Mhuire

Plan of Allangrange Church

Cawdor Church

Plan of Auldearn Church

Cille Mhuire Church

CROMARTY NH 7906/4

The late 16th century church was given a small east vestry c1700. The north transeptal aisle was added in 1739 and in 1756 the walls were heightened and new windows inserted. The north aisle was heightened in 1798. The galleries inside bear various 18th century dates, and there is a fine Mackenzie pew dated 1740. In the vestry are slabs of 1656 and 1704. In the west porch is an interesting grave-slab of c1500.

CROSSKIRK ND 025701

The tiny ruined Norman nave has doorways to the west and south but the latter is probably a later insertion. The arch towards the chancel is no wider than the doorways. The chancel itself was rebuilt as a 17th century burial enclosure. There are no windows.

CULLICUDDEN NH 648645

Only traces survive of a church of c1600 abandoned in the 1660s. More stands of a burial aisle of the Urquharts of Kinbeachie in the middle of the south side with a moulded doorway dated 1609 although the aisle itself is probably of about the time of the heraldic stone dated 1658 to John Urquhart and Isobel Cuthbert.

DINGWALL NH 550590

The easternmost of two burial enclosures north of the church of 1799 is a relic of the church of St Clement built in 1510. Under the blocked arch to the south (towards the former church) is a 15th century graveslab with black shields and a man's head.

DRUMNADROCHIT NH 505303

Only the east gable with a lancet surmounted by a shield with the initials of Alexander Grant, minister 1624-45, now survives built into a burial enclosure. The church, serving the parish of Urquhart, was probably medieval in origin but was rebuilt in 1630.

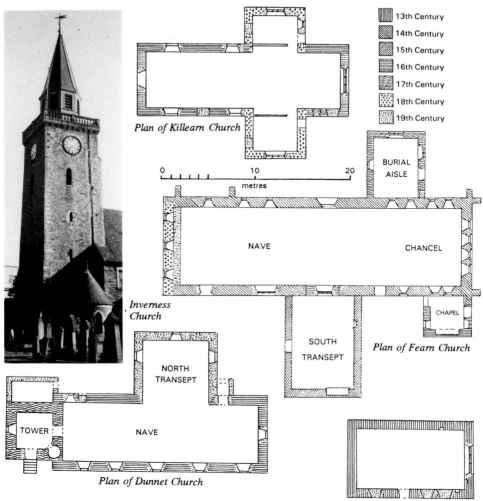

Plan of Killearn Church

13th Century
14th Century
15th Century
16th Century
17th Century
18th Century
19th Century

0   10   20
metres

BURIAL AISLE

NAVE   CHANCEL

CHAPEL

Inverness Church

SOUTH TRANSEPT

Plan of Fearn Church

NORTH TRANSEPT

TOWER   NAVE

Plan of Dunnet Church

Plan of Kilchrist Church

DUNNET   ND 220712

The main body is likely to be 16th century in origin, the blocked NW doorway being of that period. The saddleback-roofed tower could be of any period between then and the 18th century. The north aisle is of 1836 and the main body windows are 19th century.

DURNESS   NC 604669

In 1692 a north aisle with a pointed window with a mullion and transom under the crow-stepped end gable was added to a now ruined main body of 1619 containing in a recess near the SE corner the monument of its builder Duncan MacMorroch.

EDDERTON   NH 710848

A roofless mausoleum of 1637 with a moulded south door lies at the east end of the church of 1743 and 1851 handed over to the Free Church of Scotland in 1843.

EIGG   NM 488853

The roofless rectangle with small plain windows is said to have been built c1570 by John Moydartach, Captain of Clanranald. A segmental arched tomb recess is dated 1641 with the initials D.M.R. Nearby is a 14th or 15th century cross shaft carved with pairs of opposed animals and scrollwork vine patterns.

FEARN   NH 837773

Much of the large single body ashlar-faced 14th century church which served a Premonstratensian Abbey still survives, with four lancets of equal height to the east, sedilia on the south side, and pairs of lancets between buttresses in the side walls. Abbot Macfaed, d1485 added the south chapel with his effigy in a tomb recess. The chapel was refaced c1790 but is now ruined. The SE chapel may have been added during repairs in the 1540s. The east end was later walled off until the restoration of 1899 as the burial aisle of the Rosses of Balnagown, whilst in the early 17th century the Douglasses of Mulderg built themselves an aisle on the north side. After the stone-slabbed roof of the main church collapsed in 1742 its west end and the cloistral buildings were demolished to provide materials for a new church to the south. This was soon abandoned and in 1772 the old church was restored and given a new west front.

GOLSPIE   NC 831001

The church built in 1619 by Sir Robert Gordon probably incorporating parts of a medieval chapel of St Andrew was entirely replaced by a T-plan church in 1736.

INVERNESS   NH 666454

At the west end of the Old High Church of 1769-72 with porches and south apse of 1891 stands a lofty 16th century tower. It has one external offset and ends in a balustraded parapet probably of 1649 around an octagonal belfry capped by a spire.

KEILL   NM 971538

This church in Lochaber may be of c1200. There are aumbries either side of the SE corner, a south window nearby, a wider north window opposite, a west window set high up, and a wide gap corresponding to the former NW doorway.

KILCHRIST   NH 540492

The south doorway with a draw-bar slot, and the piscina and aumbry indicate a 13th century date for this chapel converted to a mausoleum c1870. The south windows, now blocked, are of later date. The church was burned by the Macdonalds in 1603.

KILLEARNAN   NH 576495

The blocked south doorway and SE window suggest a 16th century date for the main body. The transepts are of 1745. The other windows are c1800, when the heather-thatched roof was replaced by slates, and 1891. A 17th century monument lies inside.

KILMALLIE   NN 092770

West of the church of 1781 is the burial enclosure of the Camerons of Fassifern which is likely to be a former north aisle of the 16th century parish church.

KILMUIR   NH 678502

A Graham burial vault has been created in the east end of a late medieval church with a three light east window with intersecting tracery which was abandoned in 1764.

KILMUIR EASTER   NH 758723

The wide main body is of 1800. At the east end is a laird's loft dated 1616 with initials of George Munro of Milntown and Margaret Dunbar with a round spired staircase turret.

KILTARLITY   NH 497439

The ruined church of 1626 by the River Beauly has rectangular windows in the gables and two doorways in the east wall. The north wall is reduced to its foundations.

KILTEARN   NH 616653

The wide ruined main body of 1791 incorporates some medieval masonry, and jambs of the former east window can be seen. The Munros of Foulis built the aisle in 1743.

KINCRAIG   NH 825048

A mausoleum built by Captain George Mackintosh, d1780, lies in the 16th century chapel with round arched windows dedicated to St Drostan.

KINLOCHLAGGAN   NN 536897

A recess on the south is the only feature of the ivy-mantled walls of the ruined medieval church of St Kenneth. Much of the walling is a drystone replacement of the original.

KINTAIL   NG 946212

The south doorway may be 16th century or part of the repairs ordered by the Presbytery in 1649. The church was bombarded by a Hanovarian frigate in 1719 as part of the operations again Eilean Donan Castle, but was repaired in 1739. It is now a ruin. There are many monuments, most of fairly recent date, to the MacRaes.

KIRKHILL   NH 549456

The east gable of a 13th century church with traces of a large mid 14th century window inserted by Julia Ross, widow of Simon, 3rd Lord Fraser of Lovat, is incorporated into the Lovat mausoleum built in 1633 to a design by William Ross with tall round arched south windows. The gable bears an unusual belfry dated 1722 with a round top part on a square lower stage with tourelles at the corners.

Laird's loft and turret, Kilmuir Easter

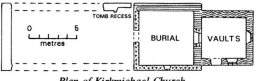

Plan of Kirkmichael Church

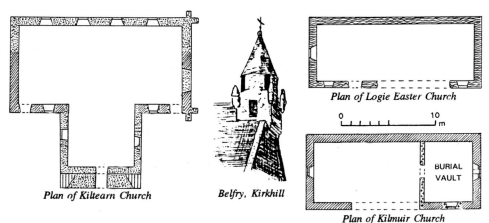

Plan of Kiltearn Church   Belfry, Kirkhill   Plan of Logie Easter Church

Plan of Kilmuir Church

BURIAL
VAULT

0   10
⌊ ⌊ ⌊ ⌊ ⌊ ⌊ ⌊ ⌊ ⌊ ⌊ ⌋ m

KIRKMICHAEL NH 706658

The chancel of a small late medieval church, disused after Resolis parish was formed in 1662, was rebuilt as the mausoleum of the Urquharts of Braelangwell. Original may be the twin lancets to the south and east. Part of the nave has been closed off as the burial place of the Munros of Poynzfield. Further west is medieval tomb recess.

LATHERON ND 203334

The church begun 1725, but mostly built in 1735-8 with a north aisle of 1821, now forms the Clan Gunn Centre. The burial aisle adjoining it containing the large monument of 1642 to Christian Mowat, wife of Sir John Sinclair of Dunbeath, has probably been created from part of the medieval church. It incorporates part of a lancet window. The pyramid-roofed bell tower on the hillside 0.5km north is probably 17th century.

LOCHALINE NM 670451 & 565538

Around the west end of the church of 1898 are a fine collection of medieval graveslabs. There are two ruinous burial enclosures on the site of transeptal aisles added to the lost 13th century church of St Columba. The north aisle has re-used 16th century parts including a fine arch on a pair of half round responds. Only traces remain of Cill Dhonnaig, Morvern's other medieval parish church, replaced by that at Fernish in 1780.

LOGIE EASTER NH 750761

The very ruined medieval church was rebuilt in 1764, a transept having been added on 1730. A 17th century church nearby is ruined and another of 1818 is now disused.

NIGG NH 805717

The main block is of 1626 probably on medieval footings. It was repaired in 1723 and given a birdcage bellcote with panelled piers and ball finials on the corners. The roof pitch was lowered in 1779-84. There is a Pictish cross-slab of c1800 inside.

NONAKILN NH 663712

Only the west wall stands above the foundations. A lintelled 17th century doorway seems to be inserted into an arched medieval opening.

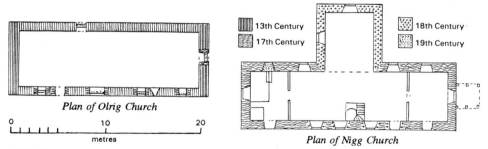

Plan of Olrig Church

▦ 13th Century	▨ 18th Century
▨ 17th Century	▩ 19th Century

0 ———— 10 ———— 20
metres

Plan of Nigg Church

OLRIG   ND 186670

The blocked north doorway and one south window are 13th or 14th century but the four south windows probably date from 1633, the year given on the NW skewputt of the ruin. There were presumably repairs in 1743, the date on the SE skewputt.

PETTY   NH 738499

At the east end of the disused church of 1836 is the Mackintosh mausoleum of c1686. It has Gothic details such as Y-tracery and has a north wing probably of 1742.

RAASAY   NG 552370

The ruined church of St Moluag with a round headed east window may be 13th century. The west gable contained three small lancets. In the SE corner is a late medieval tomb recess. A west gallery was inserted after the Reformation.

REAY   NC 967649

The present church is of 1738. The medieval church has gone but the mausoleum of 1691 of the Mackays of Bighouse which adjoins it survives. It contains a medieval slab with a Celtic cross and a tablet to Angus Mackay and Janet Sinclair.

ROSSKEEN   NH 688694

The only relics of a 17th century church reroofed with slates in 1753 are a group of burial enclosures of various dates. One has a doorway dated 1675.

SKYE   NG 255478, 376260, 617207, 436749, 225612, 658070, 484423, 497444

The Macleods of Macleod are buried in the roofless St Mary's church of 1689 at Duirinish near their seat at Dunvegan. The burial aisle on the north is dated 1735. MacLeod monuments of the 18th century lie in a late medieval chapel at Eynort which has a ruined 17th century church with several plain rectangular windows to the east. An 18th century Mackinnon burial enclosure adjoins the small ruined 16th century Cille Chriosd which has south windows checked internally for shutters. Only the west gable and foundations remain of St Martin's chapel at Kilmaluag. At Trumpan the medieval church has a mere slit for an east window. The south and east walls are reduced to footings. Beside Sleat church of 1876 is a ruin dated 1687 on the west gable. It has a round arched doorway and windows with moulded margins to the south and east. There are foundations of a chapel of St Columba on a tidal island in Portree Bay. Another chapel lay 1km NE of Portree Harbour. A gravestone showing a knight in armour remains at Kilmuir and not far away are the cashel and chapel at Loch Chalumcille.

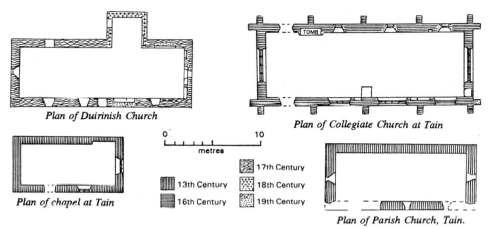

Plan of Duirinish Church

Plan of Collegiate Church at Tain

Plan of chapel at Tain

0	10

metres

17th Century

13th Century 18th Century

16th Century 19th Century

Plan of Parish Church, Tain.

TAIN   A.M.   NH 780822 & 785823

There are no less than three churches here, all of which seem to have been dedicated to St Duthus, and which were all in use in 1504. The oldest is the 13th century ruin on the links which was burnt in 1429 by McNeil of Creich during the course of a clan feud. The other two lie side by side in the town. The larger of them has windows with intersecting and geometrical tracery and heavy buttresses, although the north windows are mere lancets. A gable mark indicates there was once a large SW porch. On the south side are triple sedilia. This church served a college founded in 1487 by Thomas Hay, Bishop of Ross at the instigation of James III. James IV frequently came here on pilgrimage, and so occasionally did James V. This building ceased to be a parish church in 1815 but was restored in 1877 and is now preserved as a monument in State care. It contains an old font and a pulpit of c1575. The smaller building was perhaps built c1300. It has a triple east lancet and a double lancet and doorway to the south.

Collegiate church at Tain

Tarbat Church

TARBAT NH 915840

The west gable and footings of the main block predate the 1756 rebuilding. The north aisle enlarged in 1780 may be 17th century. The stone cupola bellcote is of c1700. A Macleod buial enclosure lies against the church and within it is a monument to William Mackenzie, d1642, and his wife, and a fragment of an heraldic tablet of c1623.

THURSO ND 117683

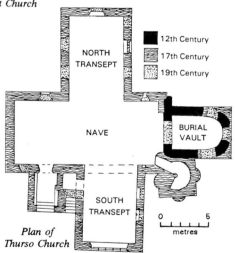

Plan of Thurso Church

The vaulted apsidal chancel (now the burial aisle of the Sinclairs of Forss) is probably 12th century work. It is square externally, perhaps as a result of mid 17th century remodelling. A square tower set diagonally with half round mid-wall buttresses was added against the south side to give access to a session house also used as the burgh court room added above the vault. By then a new nave had been raised on the footings of the medieval one and a south transept added with a south porch beside it. The north transept was added in 1664. Both nave and north transept have big end windows with Gothic tracery and the transept had a NE porch. The south transept also has a big end window and opens towards the nave a wide segmental arch. The church has been roofless since a larger new church was built nearby in 1833.

TONGUE   NC 591571

Much of the church, comprising a main body with SE and NE aisles is of 1728, but the main body is partly medieval and the south aisle doorway lintel is dated 1680. The church was repaired in 1861. The Reay Loft of 1728 is now in an Edinburgh Museum.

WICK   ND 363509

The medieval church itself has gone but there remains the north aisle added c1590 by George, 4th Earl of Caithness. It was remodelled as a burial vault in 1835 and contains a slab to Jean Chisholm, d1614, wife of Master John Sinclair of Ulbster. Further east is another vault containing the monument of Sir William Dunbar of Hempriggs, d1711.

OTHER CHURCH REMAINS IN HIGHLAND DISTRICT

ALVIE NH 864094 Mostly of 1799 but possibly with older masonry surviving.
AVOCH NH 700500 A reset Sacrement House of c1500 lies in the church of 1870.
CADBOLL NH 874769 Only buried footings remain of 13th century chapel of St Mary.
COVINTH NH 512375 Fragments and foundations only remain of wide medieval church.
CREICH NH 636892 17th century Gray burial enclosure by low walls of 1789 church.
DUNLICHTY NH 660330 Medieval masonry, features all of 1757-9, 1829, and 1859.
NAIRN NH 884566 Tablet to Rev James Dunbar, d1660 in ruined old church of 1809.
NEWTON NH 846814 Only foundations survive of a small medieval church.
SKINNET ND 132621 The lower part of the walls with two south doorways survive.
SUDDIE NH 666548 Thin fragments of late date and a 19th century vault lie on site.

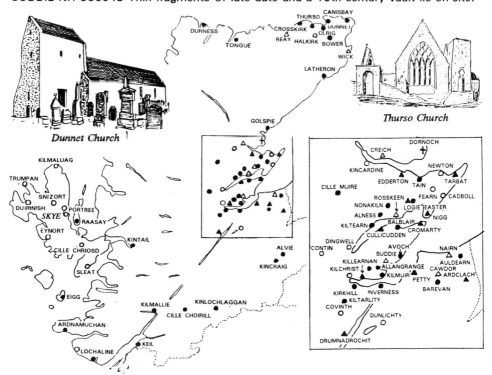

Dunnet Church

Thurso Church

LOTHIAN

ABERCORN   NT 082792

The nave and chancel form a long narrow body. They mostly date from 1579 but a blocked Norman doorway with shafts and a tympanum with a lozenge pattern survives in the nave south wall. Much of the chancel was taken by the Hopetouns as their family pew in 1708. They built a retiring room over a vault on the north, whilst adjoining the south wall is the Duddingston aisle dated 1612. In a south transeptal position is the Binns aisle and vault of 1618, and further west is the Philpston enclosure of 1727. The church was restored in 1893 and given a wide north aisle with a three bay arcade and a new west front and chancel arch. In a room under the Hopetoun aisle are fragments of two 8th century crosses, relics of an ancient monastery here, two hogback stones, two 13th century coffin lids and various other sculptured fragments.

ABERLADY   NT 462798

The 15th century west tower has a set-in top storey and a slated spire behind a corbelled parapet. Part of it once served as a dovecot. Two burial aisles of c1600 have been incorporated into the north side of the church of 1886 which has an aisle duplicating them on the south side and small porches set either side of the tower.

BATHGATE   NS 993681

The wide north doorway and the tiny NE lancet date this long plain ruin to c1200. The south doorway and east buttresses may also be original. Lying in the church is a weathered mid 13th century effigy of a priest.

BORTHWICK   NT 369596

Most of the church, including the NW tower, north transept, and vestries, is Victorian, but the nave and apse are built on foundations of a 12th century church destroyed by fire in 1775. On the south side is a blocked arch to a vaulted 15th century transept with a tomb recess containing a painted effigy of Lord Borthwick in the east wall.

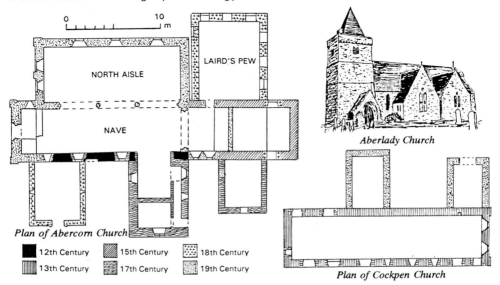

0   10
         m

NORTH AISLE

LAIRD'S PEW

NAVE

Aberlady Church

Plan of Abercorn Church

■ 12th Century	▨ 15th Century	▨ 18th Century
▥ 13th Century	▨ 17th Century	░ 19th Century

Plan of Cockpen Church

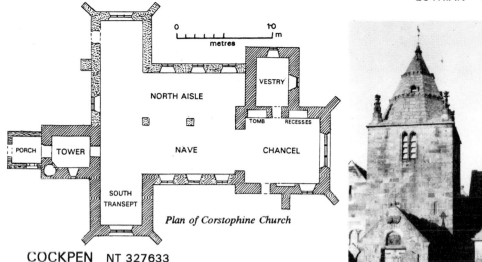

Plan of Corstophine Church

Corstophine Church

COCKPEN   NT 327633

This very overgrown ruin dates from the 13th century and has two east lancets, the other openings being straight headed. John Knox's brother William and a nephew were successively ministers here in the late 16th century.

CORSTOPHINE   NT 201728

Sir Adam Forrester built a chapel of St John the Baptist on the south side of the original parish church before his death in 1405. The present nave and the vaulted SW transept containing Sir Adam's effigy survive from that period. A college was founded in 1429, and the slab-roofed and heavily buttressed chancel wider and higher than the nave and the west tower were built after four more chaplains were added in 1444. The chancel has tomb recesses with effigies of two Sir John Forresters, d1440 and c1454, and there are slabs to Alexander Tod, d1499, and Robert Heriot, rector of Gogar, d1444. The porch is of c1650. The north aisle on the site of the original church is of 1828.

CRAMOND   NT 190769

A new church replaced a medieval ruin in 1656. The Cramond family vault lies at its east end whilst there are aisles of 1701 on either side. That on the south, once the Barnton vault, became the chancel in 1911, whilst that on the north has become part of a new nave. Inside is a cartouche to Lord James Hope, d1670.

CRICHTON   NT 381616

The cruciform church of St Mary and St Kentigern was built to serve a college founded by Sir William Crichton in 1449. The low tower extends west beyond the shallow transepts and has a saddleback roof recessed behind a parapet and plain mullioned windows. The three bay chancel has two light side windows and a four light east window. Like the transepts it has thick walls to support a plain tunnel vault. In the chancel are a piscina, Sacrement House, and three sedilia. After the Reformation the nave was destroyed except for a short section of the north wall containing the tower staircase, and the west arch of the tower was then blocked.

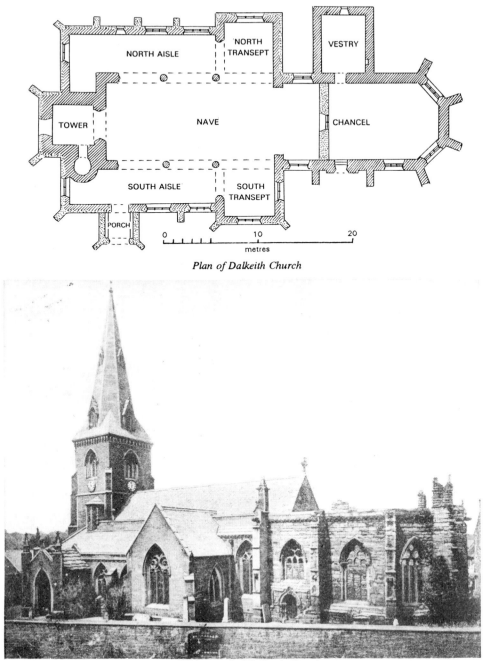

Plan of Dalkeith Church

Old postcard of Dalkeith Church

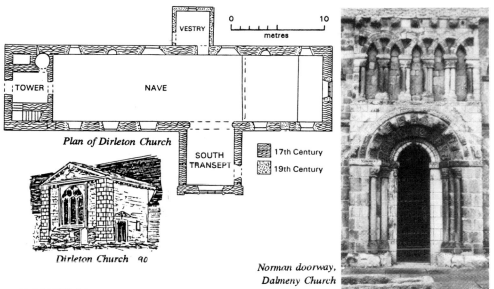

VESTRY

0 _____ 10
metres

TOWER | NAVE

Plan of Dirleton Church

SOUTH
TRANSEPT

☐ 17th Century

☐ 19th Century

Dirleton Church 90

*Norman doorway,
Dalmeny Church*

DALKEITH   NT 330670

The aisled nave and tower of St Nicholas' church date from shortly after a collegiate chapel dependant on Lasswade church was founded here in 1406. These parts have been refaced externally and the tower now has a broach spire. The church obtained full parochial status in 1467 and in c1500 was given a new three bay chancel with an apsed east end and a north sacristy, now the Buccleugh family vault. The chancel was abandoned in 1590, its vault fell, and this part remains roofless, its three light windows with loop tracery being blocked up. It contains the worn effigies of James Douglas, 1st Earl of Morton, d1400, and his wife Princess Joanna. He appears in civilian costume.

DALMENY   NT 144775

In spite of the original west tower being rebuilt in 1937 and a long north transept being added in 1671 (it was remodelled in the 19th century) this is the finest and least altered Norman parish church remaining in Scotland. It probably dates from the mid 12th century and has a nave with a fine south doorway with two orders of shafts, the signs of the Zodiac, an Agnus Dei, and other figures. Above is a section of blind intersecting arcading. The square chancel and the apse both have rib-vaults and are entered through Norman arches. They also retain original corbel tables; another on the nave was mostly destroyed when it was reroofed in 1766. The tower arch is also original and the restored windows approximate to the forms of the originals. Near the south doorway is a medieval coffin lid with a beast at one end and Christ and the Apostles on the side. It originally probably lay on the north side of the chancel.

DIRLETON   NT 513843

The long main body with a vaulted porch tower at the west end was built in 1612 to replace the remotely sited church of Gullane. The tower has a round stair turret and a straight stair in its south wall serves the gallery. The parapet was added in 1836. James Maxwell, Earl of Dirleton added in 1664 the ashlar faced south transept (Archerfield aisle) with a stone roof, a pediment, rusticated corners, and a loop-traceried window.

EDINBURGH NT 276737 etc

The church of St Giles was the only parish church in the burgh until the Reformation. It is first mentioned in 1178 (but must have existed in the 1130s) and a fine Norman doorway of three orders of arches survived on the north side until 1796. From c1370 there was a comprehensive rebuilding. An aisled nave of five bays and a central tower seem to have existed before the burning of the town in 1385 by Richard II of England. A contract survives for the building of five vaulted chapels beyond the south aisle in 1387. These formed a wide outer aisle of which only the eastern part has survived later rebuilding, a porch and a second outer aisle forming the the chapel of the Holy Blood of c1510-18 between the porch and south transept having been swept away. West of where the Norman doorway was lies the two bay Albany aisle built by Robert, Duke of Albany and Archibald, 4th Earl of Douglas as part of a penance for their part in the murder of David, Duke of Rothesay at Falkland Palace in 1401. It bears their arms and has a vaulting boss with the monogram of the Virgin. Only the east bay remains of the St John aisle of c1395 east of the former Norman doorway. Four out of the five bays of the present aisled chancel and the sacristy east of the north transept were probably complete by 1419 when the Town Council applied to have the church made collegiate. A more successful application was made in 1467 after the chancel was lengthened and given a clerestory under patronage from James II's widow Mary of Gueldres. The south transept was lengthened and between it and the chancel south aisle the Preston aisle was begun in 1455 after Sir William Preston presented an arm-bone of St Giles to the church. A boss on the tierceron vault like that over the chancel bears the arms of Patrick Hepburn, Lord Hailes, Provost of Edinburgh in 1487. A small chapel further south was added by Walter Chepman in 1507. The central tower was heightened c1460-80 and in c1500 was provided with a crown spire.

In 1560 the medieval screens and furnishings were removed. Dividing walls of c1581 allowing three separate congregations were removed while St Giles was a cathedral in 1633-8 and 1661-89, but only finally vanished in the restorations of the 1870s and 80s. In the early 19th century buildings encroaching on the outside walls were demolished and by 1833 the whole of the exterior except for the tower and spire had been refaced and some parts remodelled. Vestries and other low outer rooms were added in the 1880s. The Thistle Chapel at the SE corner was added in 1909. See plan p8.

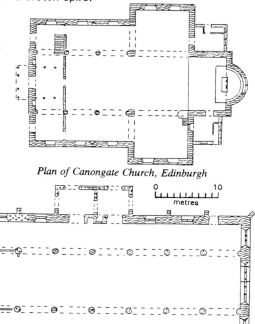

Plan of Canongate Church, Edinburgh

0   10
metres

Plan of Tron Church, Edinburgh

Plan of Greyfriars Church, Edinburgh

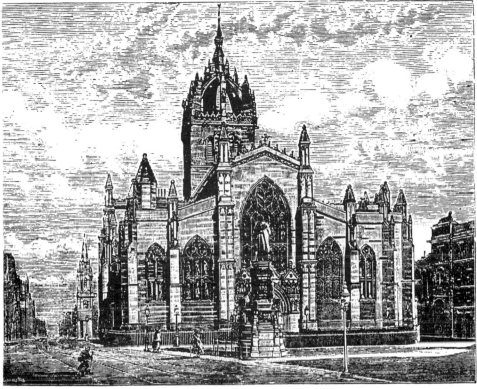

Old print of St Giles' Church, Edinburgh

Two other medieval churches built under royal patronage survive but neither served a parish. On the north side of Arthur's seat are the remains of the 14th century St Anthony's chapel (see inside of front cover). The north wall stands high and shows evidence of three bays of vaulting and domestic accommodation in a higher west end. Mary of Gueldres founded a college of the Holy Trinity in Chalmers Close c1460. It had an aisled and apsed choir and transepts with a low saddle-back roofed central tower, the nave never being built. The completed parts served as a parish church from the 1580s until 1848 when they were removed to make way for a railway. The stones were stored but many had been pilfered by 1872 when the choir alone without aisles was rebuilt on a new site between the High Street and Jeffrey Street. In Cowgate is the much altered Magdalen chapel of the 1540s with south windows and a north steeple of the 1620s which originally served a hospital founded by the MacQueen family but which was used later as the convening hall of the Incorporation of Hammermen.

The Tron Kirk begun in 1637 to a design by John Mylne was opened in 1647, although the timber "head" of the tower was not added until the 1670s. This head was destroyed by fire in 1824 and replaced four years later. In the meantime the church had been much altered from its original T-plan form with the pulpit backed onto the tower. Doorways flanking the tower were provided in 1718 and then in 1788 the aisle was replaced by a shallow recess and the east and west ends rebuilt slightly further inward than before because of improvement to the adjacent streets requiring more space. The north side had to be underpinned as part of these works.

Greyfriars church was an aisled six bay rectangle with a west tower built in 1602-4 and 1613-20 on the site of a Franciscan Friary. Originally there was a pulpit on the south side and central tables were used for communion. Here on 1638 the National Covenant was first signed in protest against Charles I's attempts to impose episcopacy back on Scotland. In the 1650s the church was divided into two by a crosswall after being occupied and mutilated by Cromwellian troops. In 1696 the galleries were enlarged and the south doorway closed up. After gunpowder stored in the tower blew up and wrecked the west end in 1718 a second cross-wall was inserted, the tower done away with and two more bays and a central half-octagonal porch added at this end. The arcades were removed and a wide open timber roof built in 1845 after a fire but in the 1930s the arcades were reinstated and the church again opened out into one. There is a splendid collection of 17th century monuments in and around the church.

The nave of Holyrood Abbey was used by the parish of Canongate until James VII closed it off as a private Roman Catholic chapel. A new church designed by James Smith and mostly paid for by a legacy from Thomas Moodie was begun c1690. It has a short chancel with an east apse and flanking vestries of the 1950s replacing originals destroyed c1850. The aisled three bay nave has Tuscan columns and transepts. A high curvilinear gable rises over the west bay with a gallery. There is a low portico with four columns, an inscription panel with a bolection moulding and the Moodie and Royal arms.

GARVALD NT 591709

The west and north walls of the main body are Norman and have a lozenge pattern on a string course. A sundial on the south wall is dated 1633, and the north transept was added in 1677. The other features date from the rebuilding of 1829.

GLENGORSE NT 245631

This ruin lies in trees on a hilltop. After a fire burial vaults with laird's lofts reached by western stairs were added to the middle of either side of a main body built in 1665. The south (Woodhouselee) loft is dated 1699. A west tower and spire were added in 1811.

GOGAR NT 168725

At the south end of the disused church of 1891 is the 16th century chancel of the old church which ceased to be used after 1602. The old east window can be still be traced.

GULLANE NT 483844

The church of St Andrew beside the Firth of Forth was abandoned for a new church at Dirleton in 1612 because the churchyard was becoming choked with sand. The Norman nave and chancel are divided by an arch with chevrons and shafts with scallop capitals. The very ruined nave, now divided into burial enclosures, was lengthened later, perhaps when a transept was added. The chancel has been extended to form another enclosure.

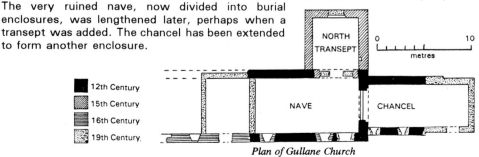

Plan of Gullane Church

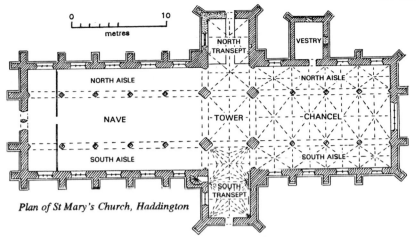

Plan of St Mary's Church, Haddington

HADDINGTON NT 518736 & 521740

The church of Mary which was under construction in the 1460s is one of the largest of its type in Scotland and lies in a spacious open graveyard. It is a fully aisled building 63m long with a four bay chancel, a five bay nave, and a low central tower with transepts. The many priests serving the chapels within the church were organised as a college c1540. Just eight years later the wooden roof of the nave and the stone vaults of the other parts were destroyed during the siege of the town by the English. The nave was subsequently repaired for worship in the Reformed manner but the other parts remained roofless until restoration in the 1970s. They were then given fibroglass vaults and the missing NW corner of the north transept was rebuilt. The plaster vault over the nave and the upper parts of the aisle walls and pinnacles were built in 1811 by James Burn. He also raised the nave arcades, which were once like those in the choir. The medieval north sacristy was converted into the Lauderdale Mausoleum in 1595 and contains a marble monument to John Maitland, Lord Thirlestane, d1595, his wife Jane Fleming, and their son John, 1st Earl of Lauderdale and his wife Isabella Seton, who both died in 1638. This part has an east window of 1877, whilst the choir has several 20th century windows. In 1682 Agnes Black erected a tabernacle to her husband William Seton, Provost of Haddington, in the south transept.

Further east is the ruined 12th century nave of St Martin's church which originally also had a chancel about 3.5m square inside. The doorways and several windows are original, but the buttresses were added later to help carry a pointed tunnel vault now destroyed.

West doorway, St Mary's Church, Haddington

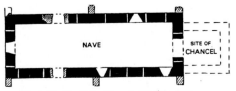

Plan of St Martin's Church, Haddington

KEITH MARISHALL   NT 448646

Hidden in trees near the house are the overgrown and ivy-covered ruins of a 13th century chancel with two east lancets, and part of a possibly still older nave.

KINNEIL   NS 988807

This 12th century church was disused by 1670 and ruined by 1740. Only the west wall with a later twin bellcote remains intact but footings of the other walls except the east end and a post-Reformation aisle opening off the chancel were exposed in 1951.

KIRKLISTON   NT 126744

Of 1190-1210 are the nave with a fine south doorway of four orders with chevrons and crocket capitals, and the west tower with clasping buttresses, tiny lancets, a battered plinth and a SE stair turret. The top storey has been cut down for a later saddleback roof. When a large north transept was added in 1883 the nave north doorway was reset in the east wall of a vestry. The original nave windows were set above a string course which the present windows all cut into. A vault and loft of 1629 adjoin the SE corner.

LASSWADE   NT 304661

A three stage west tower of c1200 with high east and west gables collapsed while under repair in 1866 and has vanished. Also then surviving was a section of the nave south wall with a round arched doorway. A 15th century high relief military effigy survives with three burial aisles formerly attached to the north wall. One belonged to the Drummonds of Hawthornden, and is the resting place of the poet William, d1649.

LEITH   NT 270761 & 263765

St Mary's chapel of c1483 at South Leith became a parish church in 1560. That same year a bombardment ruined the chancel and crossing. The nave aisles were raised to take galleries and a west steeple of 1615 was rebuilt in 1674 and demolished during a remodelling in 1847. Mills north of the river contain parts of St Ninian's chapel rebuilt in 1595 and 1736. A turret was added in 1675.

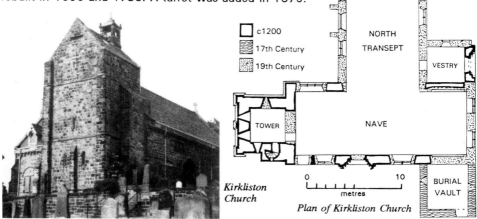

c1200
17th Century
19th Century

NORTH TRANSEPT

VESTRY

TOWER

NAVE

0   10
metres

BURIAL VAULT

Kirkliston Church

Plan of Kirkliston Church

Midcalder Church

Linlithgow Church

LINLITHGOW   NT 002773

St Michael's church lies SE of the ruined royal palace on a promontory above a loch. The five bay nave of c1440 50 replacing an older church burnt in 1424, and the three bay chancel and east apse of c1500-35 together measure 54m long. There are transeptal chapels opening off the nave eastern bay. The church was divided into two by blocking the chancel arch in the restoration of 1812, but in 1894-6 it was opened out again, the galleries removed, and a new vestry built on the site of a medieval one. The two storey porch has an oriel and a crow-stepped roof the same height as that on the south chapel. The chancel windows have loop tracery. The south chapel window is a fine specimen with a curved transom which forms with the window head a convex equilateral triangle within which three circles alternate with large dagger forms, all subdivided. The arcades are high and there are stone vaults over the aisles but only a shallow profiled plaster vault over the main span. The west tower has a polygonal NW stair turret and corner pinnacles on the embattled parapet. The aluminium spire of 1964 is a reminder of the original crown spire taken down because it was insecure c1820. In the south chancel aisle is a slab to John Forest, Provost of Linlithgow, d1589. In the vestry are two relief slabs from a late 15th century Passion retable showing the Agony in the Garden, The Betrayal, and the Mocking of Christ.

MIDCALDER   NT 074672

A thick wall carrying a belfry divides the 16th century choir from a transept of 1863. There is no nave and it is uncertain whether one ever existed. The choir has two wide bays and an apse with a rectangular vestry beyond to the east. The corbels on the north side were for the roof of the southern walk of a cloister, this being a collegiate church.

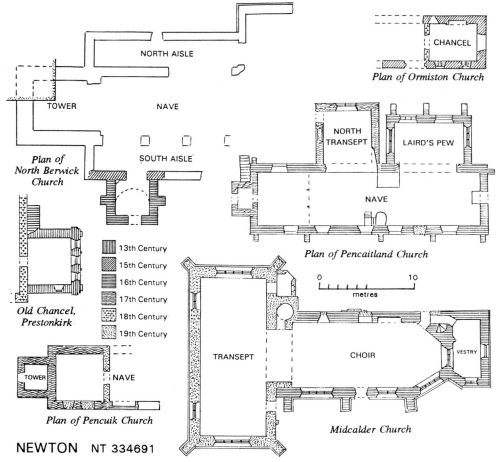

NORTH AISLE

Plan of Ormiston Church

TOWER   NAVE

NORTH
TRANSEPT   LAIRD'S PEW

Plan of
North Berwick
Church

SOUTH AISLE

NAVE

Plan of Pencaitland Church

13th Century
15th Century
16th Century
17th Century
18th Century
19th Century

Old Chancel,
Prestonkirk

0   10
metres

TOWER   NAVE

TRANSEPT   CHOIR   VESTRY

Plan of Pencuik Church

Midcalder Church

NEWTON NT 334691

When a new T-plan church was built 1km to the north the 17th century west tower of the old church was preserved as a folly visible from Dalkeith Palace to the south and was furnished with a new crenellated parapet.

NORTH BERWICK NT 554856 & 552853

Of the medieval church of St Andrew by the harbour only the 16th century porch stands complete although there are low walls and foundations of the west tower, the south aisle and three bay arcade, the 13th century north transept, and the 15th century north aisle with just a single wide arch to the nave. In Law Road is a ruined church built in 1659 and remodelled in 1770. The latter year appears along with that of 1680 on a sundial at the SE corner. It had galleries at each end, a pulpit on the north, tall windows on the south and a west tower. A new church was built by the High Street in 1882.

OLDHAMSTOCKS NT 738706

The original east wall clearly predates the Hepburn burial aisle of 1581 now converted into a chancel. The north transept, the SW corner sundial, and several doorways date from the rebuilding of 1701, whilst the windows are still more recent.

ORMISTON NT 411676

The east end is now walled off as a burial enclosure. The pointed arch on the south and the remains of the east window are clearly medieval. In the north wall is a tomb recess over which was once fixed the brass commemorating Alexander Cockburn, d1535, which is now in the National Museum of Antiquities at Edinburgh.

PENCAITLAND NT 444690

The NE chapel has late 13th century type gabled buttresses but is perhaps more likely to be later medieval. The main body is probably 16th century on medieval foundations. The north transept has initials of Sir John Sinclair on a cartouche over the mid 17th century doorway. The west tower has an octagonal top and is dated 1631 on a lintel.

PENICUIK NT 237599

A new church was built in 1771 and of the 17th century building immediately to the east there remain only the west end incorporated in a burial enclosure and the adjacent tower to which William Thomson and James Alexander added a belfry in 1731-2.

PRESTON NT 593779

At the east end of the plain St Baldred's church of 1770 with windows of 1891-2 set on a hill east of the town is the eastern part of the 13th century chancel. It was preserved because the Smeatons used it as a burial aisle. It has pilaster buttresses and three east lancets, and another to the south. The high plinth may be a later addition.

PRESTONPANS NT 388746

The octagonal belfry and most of the church date from 1774 and the north extension and east porch were added in 1911. The only relics of John Davidson's church of 1596 are the lower parts of the west tower and the west end of the south wall including a blocked doorway. On the east wall are a portrait and inscription of John Hepburn, d1675, and a stone to John Stuart of Phisgul, killed in the battle here in 1745.

RATHO NT 135706

The nave and chancel of St Mary's both have Norman cubical masonry. The nave has part of a blocked south doorway with scallop capitals and a hoodmould with sawtooth decoration. The west wall with a blocked lancet and three buttresses appears to be 13th century. The central buttress carries a belfry. The 15th century east window has no tracery but the spandrels between the heads of the lights are pierced. On the north side are two 17th century burial aisles, that to the east being dated 1683 and opening to the church in a wide segmental arch. The wide south aisle and gallery are of 1830. An 18th century gallery was removed in 1932. The 13th century tomb slab with a cross and sword possibly commemorates one of the Knights Hospitaller who then held Ratho.

RESTALRIG A.M. 283745

The 15th century main body is plain and much restored. The west wall was rebuilt in 1836. The west porch and the vestry on the site of a medieval one are of 1884. By the SW corner is the vaulted lower stage of a two storey hexagonal chapel built by James III. It was under construction from c1475 until 1487 when a college was founded. In 1962 evidence was found of an intended aisled choir never begun above the footings.

Roslin Chapel

ROSLIN A.M.* NT 275631

William Sinclair, 3rd Earl of Orkney had work begun on the church of St Matthew in the 1440s and established a college here in 1450. Only the aisled choir 10.7m wide by 21m long internally and the transept east walls were ever built of a structure designed to be 55m long. The choir has seven bays, the sixth and seventh being an ambulatory and a row of chapels respectively. To the east is a large sacristy below the level of the hill-top churchyard. Most of the building is covered with decorative carving. The piers are of complex section and have rich capitals above which are a cornice and clerestory windows with fleurons, etc, in the jambs but no tracery. The main body has a pointed tunnel vault and the aisles are covered by a series of pointed tunnel vaults set crosswise on lintels hidden behind rich encrustations. Flying buttresses help to carry the thrust of the main vault onto the aisle buttresses. In place of the intended crossing is a tall vestry and organ chamber of 1880. Monuments in the church include a mid 15th century incised slab of a knight, a tomb of George, Earl of Caithness, d1582, and a 13th century coffin lid later inscribed with the name William de Sinclair.

SETON A.M.* NT 418751

The foundations of the west end of a nave demolished in the 1580s are all that remains of a church mentioned in the 13th century. A large and massively walled south chapel was added in the 1430s by Catherine Sinclair, wife of the 1st Lord Seton. In the 1470s the 3rd Lord built a new choir of three bays with an east apse and north sacristy. A college was founded in 1492 by the 4th Lord and work continued on the choir roof until c1506. The widow of the 5th Lord killed at Flodden in 1513 had the south chapel demolished in the 1540s and the central tower and transepts then added. The spire was never finished. The transepts have windows to the west and in the end gables, but not to the east. They and the western part of the choir have pointed tunnel vaults whilst the tower and the east part of the choir have rib vaults. In the choir are fine effigies of a late 15th century knight and lady, and in the transepts are tablets to James Ogilvie of Barnes, d1617, and a splendid monument to James, Earl of Perth, c1611.

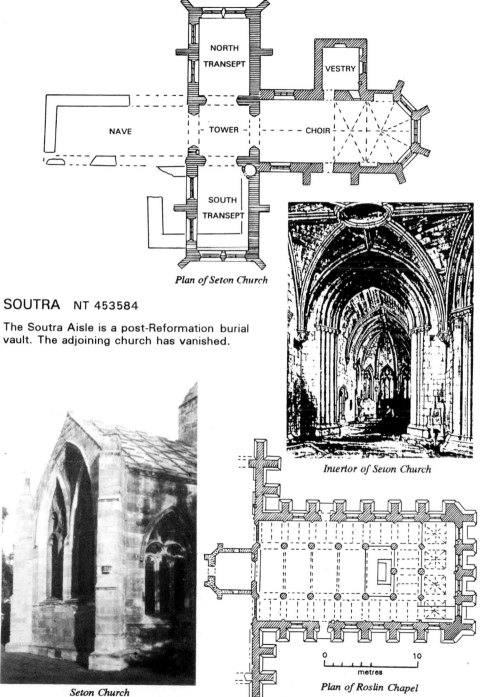

Plan of Seton Church

SOUTRA NT 453584

The Soutra Aisle is a post-Reformation burial vault. The adjoining church has vanished.

Interior of Seton Church

Seton Church

Plan of Roslin Chapel

metres

0   10

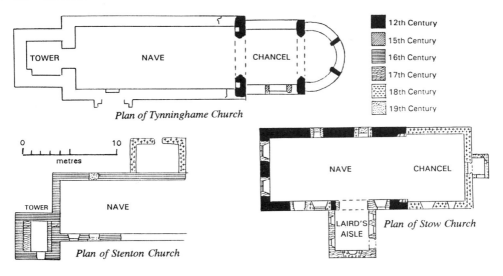

TOWER | NAVE | CHANCEL

■ 12th Century
▨ 15th Century
▤ 16th Century
▨ 17th Century
▥ 18th Century
▨ 19th Century

Plan of Tynninghame Church

0 ├──────────┤ 10
metres

TOWER | NAVE

Plan of Stenton Church

NAVE | CHANCEL

LAIRD'S AISLE

Plan of Stow Church

SOUTH QUEENSFERRY   NT 128785

St Mary's church was built in the mid 15th century to serve a Carmelite friary. It was used by the parish from the 1560s until 1633 when a new church was built in The Vennel. This latter building, which has a bird cage belfry and contains a monument to John Hutton, d1684, was restored in 1898 but has been used as offices since the 1960s. It has two blocked round headed doorways near the west end of the side walls. One Gothic window remains unaltered. The central tower, south transept, and choir of St Mary's were restored from ruin in 1890, and a west porch added where the nave demolished in 1820 had been. The choir contains numerous Dundas memorials, including a slab to George, d1600 and his wife Katherine.

South Queensferry Church

STENTON NT 623744

Projecting from the SW corner of the west end of a ruined 16th century church with a round arched south doorway is a saddleback roofed tower with crow-stepped gables.

STOW NT 458444

The main body of this church in a part of Lothian transferred to Borders Region in 1974 is partly Norman and partly of c1500, the west window of that date having loop tracery. The south transept is late 16th or early 17th century, and the east porch is dated 1799. There is a reset 13th century piscina.

TEMPLE NT 315588

The Knights Templar had their main Scottish house here from the mid 12th century until their suppression in 1312, but the surviving ruin with intersecting tracery with circles in the windows is thought to date from c1350. There are sedilia on the south side and a tomb recess on the north. The 17th century west end may be built of 12th century materials, possibly from a demolished Norman west tower.

TORPHICHEN A.M.* NS 969725

The Knights Hospitaller built a cruciform church here in c1190-1230 of which there remain the lower part of the nave north wall with the base of a doorway, the west arch of the crossing, parts of the north transept, and the foundations of the cloistral buildings. By the 15th century the church was being used by the parish and the tower and transepts were rebuilt and given rib-vaults above which are low rooms now used for historical displays. A south aisle with four arches on octagonal piers was added to the nave. The chancel was destroyed after the Reformation and a new T-plan church was built on the site of the nave and aisle in 1756. Set in the blocking wall of the west crossing arch is part of a monument to Sir George Dundas, d1532.

Temple Church

TRANENT   NT 403735

The northern part of the wide church of 1800 is built on foundations of a late 15th century church belonging to Holyrood Abbey. At the NE corner are remains of the burial aisle of the Cadells. Outside is an incised slab to the priest Alexander Crawfurd, d1489.

TYNINGHAME   NT 620798

In the grounds of the house are foundations of a Norman church dismantled after the laird cleared away the village in 1761. It comprises a west tower, a long nave with a wide and boldly projecting south doorway, a square choir and an apse. The arches to the choir and apse still stand, and also the shafts which carried the apse vault. These parts are richly ornamented with chevrons, billets, and lozenges.

UPHALL   NT 060722

The west tower, nave and chancel of St Nicholas' church all have Norman masonry. The chancel was lengthened in the 13th century and has two east lancets and another on the north, whilst on the south is a 15th century window. The Shairps of Houston added a tunnel vaulted south transept to the nave c1620, and the Buchans added a vault on the north side of the chancel in 1644. Except for the stair the latter was removed in 1878 when the north transept was added. There are Erskine memorials under the tower.

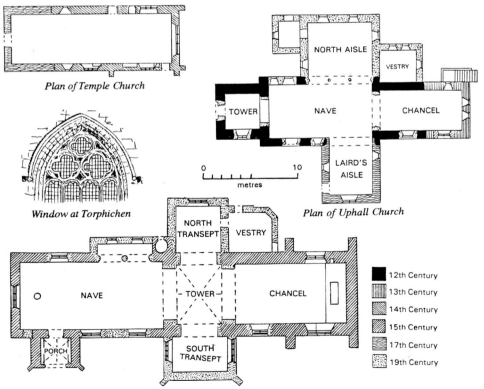

Plan of Temple Church

Window at Torphichen

Plan of Uphall Church

	NORTH AISLE	
		VESTRY
TOWER	NAVE	CHANCEL
	LAIRD'S AISLE	

0 _____ 10
metres

Plan of Whitekirk Church

NORTH TRANSEPT   VESTRY

NAVE   TOWER   CHANCEL

PORCH   SOUTH TRANSEPT

■ 12th Century
▨ 13th Century
▧ 14th Century
▨ 15th Century
▤ 17th Century
▦ 19th Century

Whitekirk Church from an old postcard

WHITEKIRK   NT 596815

In the 15th century Whitekirk was an important place of pilgrimage because of miracles of healing at a nearby well. Pilgrims' hostels were built by James I, and the church was rebuilt to a cruciform plan with a central tower. The two bay chancel with a plain pointed tunnel vault, one original south window, and a blank east wall except for a renewed oculus high up is said to be the work of Adam Hepburn of Hailes Castle in the 1430s, but the shield on the east wall is that of Abbot Crawford of Holyrood (1460-83). The north transept was rebuilt at some unknown period and the south transept was rebuilt in 1830, and again along with the crossing arches after the church was gutted by a fire started by suffragettes in 1914. Many fine 17th century furnishings were burnt. The south porch retains late medieval inner and outer arches.

YESTER   NT 545672

The 15th century collegiate church of St Cuthbert had a vaulted main body with round arches to transepts near the east end. A new east window was inserted in 1633. The 17th century pulpit was transferred to the new T-plan church built in the village of Gifford in c1710. At the old church everything west of the transepts was demolished and in 1753 the Adam brothers built a new west front for the remainder retained as the Hays' burial place. It lies hidden in shrubs near Yester House. A monument has initials of William, d1614, and Helen Cockburn, and there are floor slabs of 1566 and 1613.

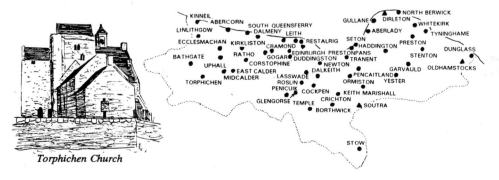

Torphichen Church

ORKNEY

BIRSAY   HY 248277

The church of St Magnus has blocked tiny 13th century lancets in the side walls, and a small blocked round headed doorway on the north. The bird-cage bellcote probably dates from the remodelling of 1664. The church was enlarged in 1760 and has a late medieval font bearing the Tulloch or Craigie arms and a worn grave slab dated 1645 with the initials NN probably referring to Nicol Nisbet.

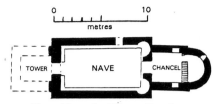

Plan of Brough of Birsay Church

BROUGH OF BIRSAY   A.M.   HY 242284

The lower parts of an early 12th century church of St Peter with apse, choir, and nave lie in a rectangular enclosure. Tusking and footings indicate that a west tower was also intended. The arch from nave to choir is only 1.3m wide and is flanked by round altar recesses. The apse arch was subsequently blocked except for a narrow doorway.

BURRAY   ND 491964

This ruin with roll mouldings on several of the windows and the SW doorway was formerly dated 1621 on a skewputt. The small SW vestry was probably added c1800.

BURWICK   ND 440843

St Mary's church, rebuilt in 1788, contains heraldric slabs to James Kynnaird of Burwick, d1624, his wife Janet Balfour, and Sir Hugh Halcro, Rector of Ronaldsay, d1544, plus an oval stone with foot shaped hollows either side of the central ridge.

DEERNESS   HY 596088

Excavations showed that the 12th century chapel of flat slabs and larger blocks was built on the site of a 10th century timber framed and stone-clad building. The site is a dramatic one on an isolated rock only reached by climbing up from the beach.

EGILSAY   A.M.   HY 466304

It is likely that the frequent visits of William, Bishop of Orkney to Egilsay in the late 1130s were to oversee the erection of the present church of St Magnus, probably on the site of an earlier building in which the saint prayed before he was killed in 1116. It consists of a nave and narrower chancel both with crowstep gables, and a round west tower with tall slit windows in the outer faces. The chancel is tunnel vaulted. The doorways and windows are mostly original but two windows in the south wall are later.

EYNHALLOW   A.M.   HY 359288

A church of c1200 comprising a nave and chancel with a pointed arch between them and a west porch perhaps intended as a tower with a round arch to the nave may have already been remodelled once before it was converted into three cottages after the Reformation. These were unroofed when the island was cleared of cottagers in 1851. Outside the nave south wall is a passage and then a wide stair in a later wing. The church may have originally served monks probably following the Benedictine rule.

Apse, Orphir

Egilsay Church

FLOTTA   ND 366931

The harled box may be 17th century in origin but in c1782 it was re-roofed with heather thatch (later replated by slates) and the round headed windows inserted.

KIRKHOUSE   ND 470908

Except perhaps for the bellcote the features of St Peter's church built in 1642 are mostly of 1801. Both these dates appear on stone over the south doorway.

ORPHIR   HY 335043

Immediately east of the church of St Nicholas is the tiny vaulted apse and a fragment of the round nave 7m in diameter of a church thought to have been built by Earl Haakon after his pilgrimage to Jerusalem c1116 and before his death c1122. Half a dozen round-naved churches inspired by the church of Holy Sepulchre at Jerusalem survive in England but this is the only known Scottish example. See page 104.

PAPA WESTRAY   HY 488527 & 487508

The chancel of the church of St Boniface is only marked by the burial enclosure of the Traills of Holland but the derelict nave still stands. It may be Norman, although the features are of 1700 (when it was extended westwards), except for a blocked slit on the north side. A hogbacked sandstone grave slab of the 12th century lies to the east. There are or were also some remains of the tiny church of St Tredwell to the SW.

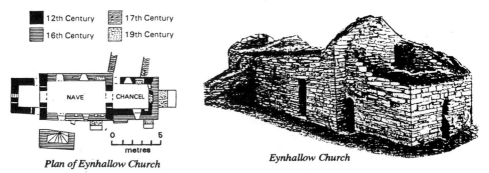

■ 12th Century   ▨ 17th Century
☰ 16th Century   ▦ 19th Century

NAVE   CHANCEL

0   5
metres

Plan of Eynhallow Church

Eynhallow Church

PIEROWALL   HY 440488

The Ladykirk was built in 1674 on the foundations of the 13th century church, and reusing its south wall. A low laird's loft corresponds to the former chancel set on a different axis to the nave. In the loft are two late 17th century stones each commemorating several Balfours and Sinclairs.

SANDAY   HY 653393 & 766399

The north wall of the Cross church at How of c1700 has been demolished. The Lady church at Silverhall is dated 1773 but inside the porch of 1902 is a west doorway with a roll and fillet moulding likely to be a survivor from a 17th century building.

SHAPINSAY   HY 502615 & NY 530186

East of the ruined church of 1822 is a roofless burial aisle dated 1656 on a lintel of the west doorway. It lay on the north side of a late 16th century church and on the arch which connected the two are the initials of Master George Buchanan of Sound. Only low walls remain of a tiny nave and chancel chapel at Linton.

STENNESS   HY 310125

Excavations in 1928 revealed the foundations of a west tower said to have been round towards the west, although rising from a square base.

TUQUOY   HY 455432

The low segmental vaulted chancel and the nave of Crosskirk are both Norman. The nave has a round headed doorway and window on the south side. The west end was later extended and provided with a second southern doorway.

WYRE   NY 444264

Near the mid 12th century Cubbie Roo's castle is a small chapel of about the same date. The arch between the nave and the chancel is just 0.7m wide.

OTHER CHURCH REMAINS IN ORKNEY

COSTA HY 337287 Footings of small nave and chancel.
GRAEMSAY HY 257046 2m high ruin beside later church.
ROUSAY HY 373304 late 16th century ruin at Skaill.
ST MARY HY 310145 Only foundations now remain.

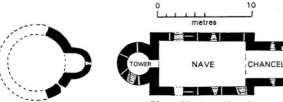

Plan of Orphir Church   *Plan of Egilsay Church*

SHETLAND

BRESSAY HU 522423 Lower walls of the cruciform church of St Mary at Cullingsburgh. The graveslabs include those to Agnes Gifford, d1628, and Claes Jansen Bryn d1636.

CROSSKIRK HU 213780 Only the lowest couses remain of a medieval single rectangle with a west doorway at Esha Ness.

DELTING HU 405638 Roofless early 18th century T-plan church with two doorways in the middle of the south wall. North aisle has a large segmental arched entrance with arms and initials of Thomas Gifford of Busta & Elizabeth Mitchell with the date 1714.

HAROLDSWICK HP 648124 Only the lower parts of the walls survive of the nave of the Crosskirk at Clibberswick. Traces of a tiny chancel have been found.

LUNDA WICK HP 566042 12th century chapel with original west doorway and small window in each side wall. East end rebuilt later on old foundations.

LUNNA HU 486691 East of the harled church of 1753 containing the Hunter family memorials are buttresses forming the side walls of burial enclosures. One has a squint which may be a relic of a medieval church here.

MID YELL HU 515907 Fragments of the old parish church include a round arched west doorway, perhaps 17th century. There are burial enclosures against the north wall.

NORTH YELL HP 532050 Excavations have revealed the lower parts of the nave and chancel. The chancel has an aumbry and two windows on one side and a recess and another window on the other. The nave has a blocked SW doorway.

ST NINIANS HU 368208 Excavations in 1955-9 revealed the footings of a small 12th century nave to which a narrower chancel was later added. Here was found a hoard of Pictish silver objects, hidden from the Vikings c800 and now at Edinburgh.

SAND HP 618028 In a graveyard beside the shore lies a ruined late medieval nave with a segmental arch into a narrower chancel now only marked by loose boulders.

TINGWALL HU 419438 SE of the harled church of 1788 is a turf covered mausoleum thought to be part of the previous church. The roll-moulded doorway looks 17th century. Inside are various 17th and 18th century grave-slabs, the most notable being that of Thomas Boune, d1603.

UYEA HU 608985 The tiny ruined window-less 12th century nave has a blocked west doorway to a later sacristy of large stones with a blocked north door and a jamb of a west window. The arch to a vanished chancel is no wider than a doorway.

UYEASOUND (GLETNA) HP 593021 Fragments remain of a rectangular medieval church with a west doorway.

Plan of Lunda Wick Church

Plan of Uyea Church

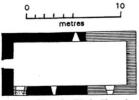

Plan of Lunda Wick Church

Plan of Cullingburgh Church

TAYSIDE AND CENTRAL SCOTLAND

ABERUTHVEN NN 983152

The two small ogival headed windows in the east wall of the ruined church of St Kattans SW of the village suggest a 15th century date. The join in the north wall marks the extent of a Norman nave. Part is now roofed as burial enclosures.

AIRLIE NO 313516

The present church mostly dates from 1781 but in the east vestibule is a sandstone pre-Reformation aumbry with a depiction of the Five Wounds of Christ.

AIRTH NS 901849

Beside the castle are the shamefully neglected ruins of a church of some interest. The blocked arch to the Bruce burial aisle of 1614 is actually the surviving easternmost arch of a late 12th century arcade of three bays with waterleaf capitals on the round piers. On the south side of the nave is a transeptal chapel built in 1450-87 by Alexander Bruce of Airth which contains a female effigy of c1330, and west of it is a laird's aisle dated 1593 on the gable with initials of Alexander Elphinstone and Jane Livingstone. It contains seven heraldic grave slabs of 1593-1638 and is entered by a west doorway. The nave west wall was rebuilt sometime in the 17th century. The chancel of 1647 has on the south side a tower built against the Airth aisle and a set of outside steps, whilst on the north side is a aisle with a three bay arcade of round arches on square piers with the corners rounded. See the picture of the church interior on the back of the cover.

ALDBAR NO 573583

Deep in the Den of Aldbar is a laird's burial enclosure which is all that remains of a church which served the former parish of Aldbar suppressed in the 17th century.

ALYTH NO 246484

All that remains of the church is the chancel south wall with 12th and 15th century features, plus the three bay arcade between the nave and the 16th century south aisle.

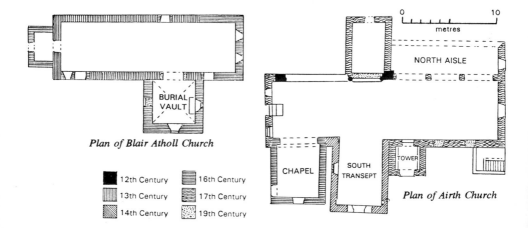

Plan of Blair Atholl Church

0   10
metres

NORTH AISLE

■ 12th Century	▦ 16th Century
▥ 13th Century	▨ 17th Century
▧ 14th Century	░ 19th Century

CHAPEL   SOUTH TRANSEPT   TOWER

Plan of Airth Church

AUCHTERARDER   NN 953140

Only a small tower remains of the 17th century church in the village. It is approached by a set of steps and has the marks of the roofs of two successive churches of different widths. Far to the NE are the overgrown and featureless remains of the church of St Mackessock, founded at the end of the 12th century by Gilbert, Earl of Strathearn.

AUCHTERHOUSE   NO 343382

Much of the church dates from 1775 but there is an old font, a 17th century south doorway, and an eastern burial aisle of 1630 now used as a chancel.

BALQUIDDER   NN 536210

Tower at Auchterader

The medieval church lay beside the position of the celebrated graves of Robert Macgregor (Rob Roy), d1734 aged about 70, his wife Mary (Helen) and his sons Coll and Robert. The ruin to the west is of 1613 and later. Much of the north and west walls have gone but there remain windows and doorways of late date in the south wall.

BARRY   NO 535345

Inside the ruined church mostly rebuilt in 1818 is a renewed panel dated 1664 with the arms of Grizel Durham and David Alexander.

BENDOCHTY   NO 218415

Although said to be 13th century the existing church appears to be mostly of 1885. Inside is a slab depicting John Cumming of Couttie, d1606, and stones referring to Donal Campbell, former Abbot of Coupar, d1587, and Leonard Leslie, Commendator of Coupar, who died in 1605 at the ripe old age of 81.

BLAIR ATHOLL   NN 867665

In the castle grounds lies a ruined century church in which is buried John Graham of Claverhouse, mortally mounded at the nearby Battle of Killiecrankie in 1689. The church existed in 1275 and in c1475 was the scene of the capture of the Earl and Countess of Atholl during a raid by Angus of Islay. The burial vault on the south side contains an incised slab and once bore the Murray arms and the date 1579.

BRECHIN   NO 600602 &

The south wall with a doorway and three large lancets alone remains of a late medieval chapel known as Maison Dieu which served a hospital. The 13th century cathedral with transepts rebuilt in the 19th century now serves as the parish church.

CAMPSIE   NS 610797

Of the church of St Machan once said to be 23m long there remain only the west wall with a 17th century doorway and stepped gable, and part of the north wall.

Dargie or Invergowrie Church

CARMYLIE   NO 548426

The church has been reorientated by the Victorians with a big north extension. The west aisle is dated 1670 and the east aisle and south end wall of the main block are also 17th century work probably built on the foundations of the medieval St Mary's.

COLLACE   NO 197320

An arched doorway with dog-tooth moulding is included in a fragment of the medieval church made into a mausoleum to the Nairnes of Dunsinnan by the church of 1813.

CRIANLARICH   NN 358284

A broken font lies beside the part of the south wall of the church of St Fillan which stands high with ragged holes for a doorway and window. Otherwise only foundations remain. The building was quite large and may have served a small monastery.

DARGIE   NO 351301

The small ruined church has a late medieval south doorway and window. Two 18th century burial aisles adjoin the north wall. A pair of fragmentary stones go back to the period of St Boniface, who landed here at Invergowrie in c715.

DUNDEE   NO 402302

St Mary's church was founded by David, Earl of Huntingdon in the 12th century and was burnt by the English in 1296, 1385 and 1547. It was rebuilt as a large cruciform structure in the 15th century. Of this there remains only the lofty west tower with a west doorway of two round openings under a another round arch. The basement served at one time as a prison. The tower was defended against General Monck in 1650, its garrison being eventually smoked out and massacred. By that time the church had been divided into three separate places of worship. St Clement's church in the former nave was rebuilt in the 18th century. St Paul's on the site of the former transepts dates from 1847, and the town church of St Mary on the site of the choir dates from 1844.

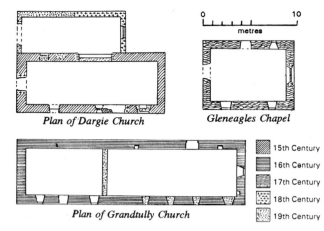

Plan of Dargie Church

Gleneagles Chapel

Plan of Grandtully Church

15th Century
16th Century
17th Century
18th Century
19th Century

Dunning Church

DUNNING   NO 019145

The church of St Serf has a fine lofty 12th century west tower with a saddleback roof, two light belfry openings and a staircase in the SW corner. There is a plain pointed arch to the nave which is also partly Norman on the north side where there is a blocked doorway and remains of the corbel table. An outside stair at the east end leads to a doorway dated 1687, but much of the main body is of 1819 and later.

EASSIE   NO 353474

The ivy-clad ruin is of uncertain date and little interest in itself but it contains a very fine 8th or 9th century Pictish cross-slab.

ECCLES   NS 796916

The 16th century chancel with a 17th century burial aisle to the north and a tower remain of the church of St Ninian which was used as a powder magazine in 1746 and was blown up. The 15th century nave has gone. A church of 1750 lies to the east.

ECCLESIAMAGIRDLE   NO 107163

The small ruined chapel hidden in dense foliage on the estate may be of early date. It has been much restored and altered into a burial enclosure.

EDZELL   NO 582688

The only relic of St Laurence's church is the Lindsay burial aisle incorporating a piscina and representing, or built of the materials of, the former medieval chancel.

ETHIE   NO 705480

Just one featureless gable remains of the cliff-top church of St Murdoch. Despite its remote situation far from any road this was once the parish church of Ethie.

FALKIRK   NS 887800

Only the 15th century southern crossing piers now supporting a tower of 1734 by William Adam survive of the cruciform medieval church of St Modan first mentioned in the late 11th century. Among the monuments inside are effigies thought to be Sir Alexander Livingstone or his son James and William 6th Lord Livingstone d1592 with their wives. In the graveyard are slabs to Sir John de Graham and Sir John Stewart of Bonkle, both killed in the nearby battle in 1298. There is a fragment of a cross head.

FORGANDENNY   NN 088184

The masonry of the main body is likely to be medieval and the south wall has a reset fragment of a Norman arch with chevrons. Two Norman windows were traced in the east wall c1880. The existing windows are fairly recent. The laird's loft on the south is 17th century. A shield and the date 1718 appear on the nave SW corner.

FOWLIS EASTER   NO 322335

The church of St Marnock first mentioned in 1180 was rebuilt in 1453 by Andrew Grey, d1469. It is ashlar faced and has a fine four light west window, a round headed south doorway with an ogival hood-mould and several other plain south windows. The only north window helped light the loft upon the former screen which divided the church. A loose doorway from the loft still survives. Other features of interest are the jougs by the doorway, the mutilated font, a Sacrament House adorned with a scene of the Annunciation, and four late medieval paintings on oak depicting the Crucifixion, The Virgin, St John The Baptist, and St Catherine. There is a cross-slab lying outside.

FOWLIS WESTER   NN 928240

The long main body probably has medieval masonry and there are several blocked openings likely to be of the 16th and 17th centuries. The north aisle is of uncertain date. The present windows are 19th century.

Fowlis Wester Church

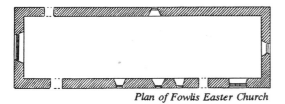

Plan of Fowlis Easter Church

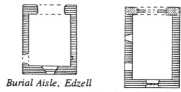

Burial Aisle, Edzell

Burial Aisle, Guthrie

GLAMIS   NO 386469

Nothing remains of the church of St Fergus consecrated in 1242 and built on a site thought to have been in use since c750. There is a fragment of a cross-slab in the present church which has the plain Strathmore family burial-vault of uncertain age lying at the NE corner.

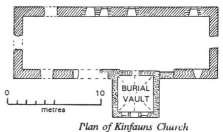

Plan of Kinfauns Church

GLENEAGLES   NN 930090

The small existing building is of uncertain age and purpose. It be a burial aisle built from relics of a medieval church. The east window cuts into the gable. The side windows have wooden shutters in the lower half of the openings and glass above.

GLENPROSEN   NO 319668

Hidden away on a tree-clad hillside in this remote valley is a ruined church of uncertain date with a small square turret projecting from the SW corner.

GRANDTULLY   NN 886506

Much of the masonry of the church of St Mary built in 1533 may remain, but there was considerable rebuilding in 1636. The present doorway is in the north wall and all the southern openings east of a modern crosswall are blocked. The exterior is whitewashed.

Gleneagles Chapel

GUTHRIE   NO 567505

This was an ancient foundation and was eventually made collegiate. The main body was rebuilt in 1826 but there survives the south transept dated 1479, now the Guthrie family burial place. It was added by Sir David Guthrie after he purchased the patronage from Arbroath Abbey and has a moulded mullioned south window and an old font.

INCHBREAOCH   NO 707568

The church of St Brioc was ruinous by 1573. A burial enclosure of the Scotts of Rossie on the site may incorporate material from it.

INCHCAILLEACH   NS 410906

Foundations of a nave and chancel church of the late 12th or early 13th century on an island in Loch Lomond were excavated in 1903. The church was abandoned in 1621.

INNERPEFFRAY   A.M. NN 184184

This long low building with a plinth all round was built as a collegiate church by Lord Drummond in 1508. A chapel of St Mary here is mentioned in 1342. The doorway and squint on the north side mark the site of a destroyed vestry. The western end has a room above with a fireplace in the end gable. It is reached by a spiral stair in the NW corner. Three corbels on the inner south wall are probably relics of a former rood loft and screen removed at the Reformation. Beside the church is the celebrated library.

INVERKEILOR   NO 664496

The main body appears to be all of 1830 and 1862 and the north transept is of 1735, but the roofless Northesk aisle or Carnegie family vault at the east end is older, having heraldic panels with the date 1636.

Innerpeffray Church

Kilmadock Church

KILMADOCK   NO 732021

The church of St Bean was intact although roofless until the 19th century. Only the east wall with a later doorway below a medieval lancet now survives by two burial enclosures. The church was repaired in 1680.

KINFAUNS   NO 166223

The rib-vaulted 15th century south transept survives as the burial place of the Charteris and Grey families. It has been much rebuilt and altered. The main body has a roll-moulded north doorway. See the plan on page p111.

KINKELL   NN 937163

The ruined church of St Bean is likely to be medieval but there are now no features older than the SE skewputt bearing the date 1701.

KIPPEN   NS 651948

The west gable of a post-Reformation church is incorporated in a burial aisle. The church was rebuilt in 1691, 1737, and 1779 and succeeded an earlier church probably located elsewhere.

KIRKINTILLOCH   NS 655740

The medieval church was replaced in 1644 by an equal armed cross with one gable having a belfry and the other three crow-stepped with large pointed windows with mullions and transoms. The church is now abandoned.

LOGIE   NS 815969

The church is first mentioned c1178. It was 17m long and had a north aisle. Only a part of the west gable remains, with a window sill dated 1598 and a sundial of 1678.

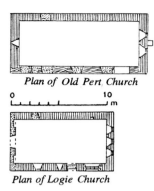

Plan of Old Pert Church

0   10
L   m

Plan of Logie Church

Logie Church

LOGIE NO 665493

The 13th century chancel with three east lancets is still roofed but derelict. The SW window and the aumbry of a sacrement house near the NW corner are late-medieval. The west wall in place of the former chancel arch dates only from 1857.

LUNDIE NO 291366

The north wall of the small church of St Lawrence has a narrow lancet of c1200 and two blocked 18th century windows. The west wall is also ancient but much else dates from 1847. An east apse was removed in 1786.

METHVEN NO 025260

The church of St Marnoch consecrated in 1247 was made collegiate by Walter Stewart, Earl of Atholl, d1437, and remained in use until 1783. There were two 16th century transepts of which the northern survives. It has a blocked three light north window with reticulated tracery and brackets for long lost statues.

MONCRIEFF NO 138193

An apse and transepts were added in the late 19th century to a small ivy-clad rectangular chamber in trees with a doorway and two windows in the south wall, a window facing west, a tiny chapel on the north side and an aumbry near the NE corner.

MOULIN NN 944592

The church has a lintel dated 1613. In was enlarged in 1704 and remodelled in 1787. In the churchyard are two slabs carved with swords. One also has a Maltese cross.

MUTHILL NN 869170

The high saddleback roofed Norman tower now lies within the western end of the aisled nave built in 1430 by Michael Ochiltree, Dean of Dunblane. The belfry windows are 17th or 18th century. The south arcade is independent of the tower and has three arches. The northern arcade joined to the tower has only two. The outer walls are thin and are much reduced on the north side. The south aisle windows may be 15th century although the doorway is probably 17th century. There are only slight remains of the long unaisled chancel destroyed after the Reformation as superfluous to requirements.

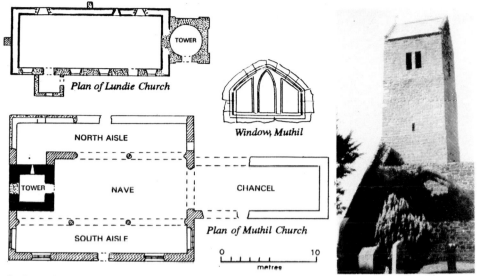

Plan of Lundie Church

NORTH AISLE

TOWER

NAVE

CHANCEL

SOUTH AISLE

Window, Muthil

Plan of Muthil Church

0   10
metres

Muthil Church

OLD NEVAY   NO 312441

The tiny roll-moulded west window is probably 16th century but the other openings are likely to be later. The date 1597 appears on a slab.

OLD PERT   NO 644660

The two east windows, the single west lancet, and perhaps also the doorways of the ruin are original 13th century work. The blocked south windows are 17th century.

PERTH   NO 115234

The church of St John the Baptist is first recorded in 1126, a newly built part of it was consecrated in 1242, and in the church was buried the heart of Alexander III in 1286. However the earliest part of the present building is the chancel which is referred to as new in 1448. The vaulted central tower, the transepts and the nave took their present form in subsequent decades. Both nave and chancel are fully aisled and of five bays, the overall length of the building being nearly 60m. The chancel has square arcade piers with half-round shafts and the walls are buttressed between the windows of four lights. There are doorways in shallow projections in the second bay from the west. The nave lacks buttresses and has two-light windows and octagonal piers. The north doorway, covered by a porch is in the second bay, whilst the south doorway lies in the middle bay. There are indications of a chapel in the angle between the north transept (which has been rebuilt shorter than before to contain a War Memorial) and the eastern bay, and it is known there was once a similar chapel on the south side, perhaps the chapel of St James which was rebuilt c1400 after becoming ruinous. In 1559 John Knox preached in St John's to such effect that a mob descended on the religious houses of the district and ravaged them. St John's itself was stripped of its furnishings and monuments and reduced to an empty shell. It was described in 1585 as in a "ruinous, pitiful, and lamentable state", but was only repaired in 1598, being divided into three separate churches. Not until the 1923 restoration did the building become a single church again. The lead covered spire was rebuilt in 1617, the original having been blown away in a gale in 1610.

St Vigeans Church

Plan of Strowan Church

St Fillans Church

ST FILLANS   NN 704237

The roofless shell remains of a small and plain rectangular box probably dating from the 16th or 17th century. A lintelled doorway and window lie on the south side.

ST VIGEANS   NO 638429

Parts of the end walls remain of the simple rectangular 12th century church. There was a fresh consecration in 1242 after the addition of a south aisle with a tower projecting to the west. The arcade between the nave and aisle was later moved northwards and they exchanged roles. This may have coincided with the addition of a fresh south aisle with a four bay arcade prior to another consecration in 1485. The eastern apse, outer north aisle and the windows are all of the time of the restoration of 1872. Inside is a monument to Sir Peter Young, tutor in the 1580s to the teenage James VI.

Stirling Church from an old postcard

STIRLING   NS 793936

The original 12th century church was repaired in 1414 after being burnt. It suffered more damage in 1455 during James II's contest with the Douglasses, and the king then provided funds for building the present five bay nave and aisles and the lower stage of the rectangular west tower. Both aisles and tower have octopartite rib-vaults. The easternmost arcade piers are lozenge shaped but the others and the responds are round. In the 1480s wealthy burgesses began to erect chantry chapels beyond the aisles but only blocked arches and footings remain of most of them. In 1507 work on the choir was begun but it dragged on until the 1540s, by which time the church had been made collegiate. The choir has three bays flanked by vaulted aisles with four light windows and a polygonal apse of two bays with huge buttresses. Piers were begun but left incomplete for a central tower which was given up and the west tower built up instead. A controversy over the appointment of a second minister in 1656 led to the erection of a partition wall for separate congregations. There were restorations in 1803, 1818, 1869, and 1911-4, but not until 1936-40 were the two parts reunited as one church and the intended transepts finally erected.

STROWAN   NN 821210

The eastern half remains of a probably medieval church with windows of later date in the south and east walls.

TULLIBARDINE   A.M. NN 900134

Reset on the church are panels referring to Sir David Murray, d1452, who founded a college here in 1446. The main body of the church with a finely moulded south doorway must be his work whilst the small west tower and the transepts with flowing tracery in their end windows are additions of c1500 by Sir Andrew Murray and his wife Margaret Barclay. These later parts have masons' marks on their arches. The south transept has a segmental arch to the nave and is somewhat irregularly laid out. The college was suppressed in the 1560s and the church ceased to serve a parish in 1745 but was retained as a Murray burial place until taken into State care.

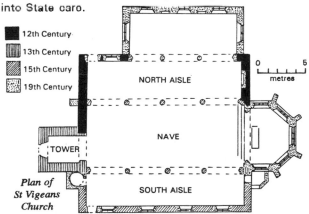

Plan of St Vigeans Church

- 12th Century
- 13th Century
- 15th Century
- 19th Century

NORTH AISLE

NAVE

TOWER

SOUTH AISLE

0 ____ 5
metres

Tower at Stirling

Tullibardine Church

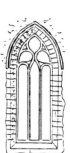

Window at Tullibardine

TULLIBODY   NS 860954

The moulded mullioned window may be of 1539, the date that appears on the ruin. The porch and south windows may also be 16th century. The west window is later.

WAST TOWN   NO 240275

A 16th century nave survives with at the east end a blocked arch which once led into a chancel or burial aisle of similar width.

WEEM   NN 844498

The church contains a fine early rennaissance monument and has roll-mouldings to the windows and doorways, one of the latter being dated 1609 with the arms of Menzies and Campbell. The monument and hatchments inside after refer to the Menzies family. The north aisle is probably a later 17th century addition.

OTHER CHURCH REMAINS IN TAYSIDE AND CENTRAL SCOTLAND

ALLOA NS 884926 Only the west tower and adjoining parts of the nave survive.
ARNGASK NO 139108 Ivy-covered ruin in woods near house. Burial place of Balvairds.
BENVIE NO 295324 Only the thick west wall of the small church now remains standing.
BOTHKENNAR NS 903834 Church of 1673, widened in 1789, with additions of 1887.
CAMBUSMICHAEL NO 115326 Single chamber with a tiny south window and doorway.
CARESTON NO 528603 17th century T-plan with laird's loft and vault on north side.
CUMBERNAULD NS 758748 St Ninian's is of 1659, but was restored in 1810.
FINTRY NO 411330 Burial aisle formed from or on site of chapel by Mains Castle.
INVERMARK NO 432803 Featureless remains probably of the 17th century.
KILBRYDE NN 756027 A mausoleum of 1864 appears to have older work in north wall.
KINNOULL NO 134218 Burial aisle with fine monument of 1st Earl of Kinnoull, d1635.
KIRKDEN NO 527480 Scanty remains of a church on a knoll near Letham.
LETHNOT NO 546685 The ruined church of 1827 has thick older gable walls.
LOGIE ALMOND NO 010299 Featureless remains of small church of uncertain date.
NAVAR NO 528676 Belfry survives among undergrowth. Remainder dismantled c1725.
ST BRIDE NN 585099 Only foundations remain of a small medieval chapel-of-ease.

Last remains of St Bride's Chapel

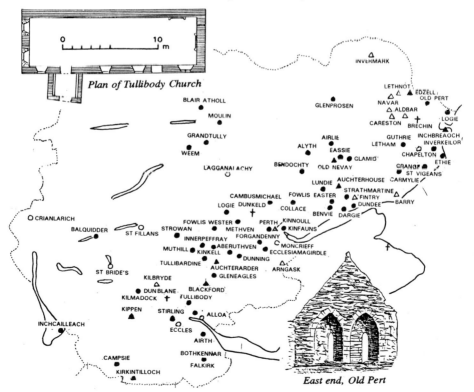

Plan of Tullibody Church

INVERMARK

LETHNOT
EDZELL
OLD PERT
BLAIR ATHOLL   GLENPROSEN   NAVAR   ALDBAR
NAVAR
CARESTON   BRECHIN   LOGIE
MOULIN
AIRLIE   GUTHRIE   INCHBREAOCH
GRANDTULLY   ALYTH   EASSIE   LETHAM   INVERKEILOR
WEEM   CHAPELTON
LAGGANALACHY   BENDOCHTY   OLD NEVAY   GLAMIS   ETHIE
GRANGE   ST VIGEANS
LUNDIE   AUCHTERHOUSE   CARMYLIE
CAMBUSMICHAEL   FOWLIS EASTER   STRATHMARTINE
LOGIE DUNKELD   COLLACE   FINTRY   BARRY
BENVIE   DUNDEE
CRIANLARICH   FOWLIS WESTER   DARGIE
BALQUIDDER   ST FILLANS   STROWAN   PERTH KINNOULL
METHVEN   KINFAUNS
INNERPEFFRAY   FORGANDENNY
MUTHILL KINKELL   ABERUTHVEN   MONCRIEFF
DUNNING   ECCLESIAMAGIRDLE
TULLIBARDINE   AUCHTERARDER   ARNGASK
GLENEAGLES
ST BRIDE'S   KILBRYDE
DUN BLANE   BLACKFORD
KILMADOCK   TULLIBODY
KIPPEN   STIRLING   ALLOA
INCHCAILLEACH   ECCLES
AIRTH
CAMPSIE   BOTHKENNAR
KIRKINTILLOCH   FALKIRK

East end, Old Pert

THE WESTERN ISLES

BARRA   NF 705074

Of the 12th century church of St Barr there remain the partly rebuilt south wall with two round headed windows with triangular rere-arches and the north wall with another window of this type and a round arched doorway later given two slanting lintels. The 15th century chapel to the SE has a small window with a lintel carved as a round headed arch. A 16th century NE chapel has been reroofed to protect four late medieval grave-slabs and a cast of the 10th Kilbar Stone which has on one side a cross with plaits and the other runes stating that it commemorates Thorketh, daughter of Steinar.

BENBECULA   NF 782549 & 766537

The thinner walls of the chancel of Teampull Chaluim Chille (St Malcolm's Church) suggest that it is a later addition to the nave. Both are much ruined and the east gable has gone. There are small rectangular side windows and a narrow western doorway. The small ruined chapel at Nunton has a niche for a statue over the west doorway.

BRAGAR   NB 288489

There are only slit windows in the ruined late medieval nave and chancel church of St John. South of the chancel are footings of an L-planned building of later date.

ENSAY   NF 981866

The small late medieval chapel has a single narrow loop in each wall (another on the north is blocked), a south doorway, and a step for the altar at the east end.

EUROPIE   NB 519652

St Moluag's Church of c1200 has a round headed SW doorway and round arched windows on all sides, that at the east having a pointed rere-arch. The north windows are placed high up. Recesses in the side walls suggest the position of the rood-beam. The end walls have plinths, that on the west returning for a short way along the side walls. Of slightly later date are the north sacristy and the SE chapel with slit windows.

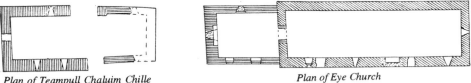

Plan of Teampull Chaluim Chille   *Plan of Eye Church*

Old postcard of Teampull Chaluim Chille, Benbecula

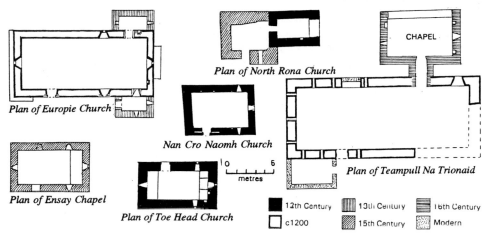

Plan of Europie Church

Plan of North Rona Church

CHAPEL

Nan Cro Naomh Church

Plan of Teampull Na Trionaid

Plan of Ensay Chapel

Plan of Toe Head Church

metres

■ 12th Century ▦ 13th Century ▤ 16th Century
□ c1200 ▨ 15th Century ░ Modern

EYE NB 482322

In c1500 a west chapel with round arched and rectangular windows and a tomb recess and south doorway (both round arched) was added to a 14th century main body with slit windows. The original round headed south doorway was then blocked and a new doorway made to the east, whilst the doorway and high set window further west are probably 17th century. Fixed on the south wall of the ruin is a slab with a life-sized relief of a knight of c1400. On the north wall is a slab carved with foliage and animals to Margaret MacLeod, d1503. A third medieval slab with a sword lies on the ground.

GALSTON NB 433594

The small half-buried church of the Holy Blood (Teampull Nan Cro Naomb) may be 12th or 13th century. A small window and a SW doorway survive in the south wall, and there is a larger rectangular north window. Little remains of the end walls.

GRESS NB 490416

The small roofless chapel with a panel over the door with the initials I.B. and M.K. and the date 1681, contains medieval work and is said to have been dedicated to St Olaf.

GRIMSAY NF 883547

The west gable and footings of the other walls remain of a small chapel of St Michael.

NORTH RONA HW 809323

The original 8th or 9th century chapel of the hermit St Ronan measuring just 3.5m by 2.4m and originally roofed with slabs of gneiss later became a chancel serving a wider medieval nave with a south wall rebuilt in 1938 which is 1.5m thick in its eastern section. The church lies on a remote island far to the NE of the Butt of Lewis.

NORTHTON NF 970714

Each wall of the small ruined chapel contains a slit window, that at the west being placed higher up. There are steps at the end, that on the east with the seating for the altar. Beside this is a corbel for a statue and a pair of aumbries.

NORTH UIST   NF 816603

The early looking masonry suggests that the present ruin of Holy Trinity (Teampull Na Trionaid) may be the church said to have been built c1200 by Bethoc, daughter of Somerled. A vaulted passage on the north side links it to a 16th century building with rectangular windows and aumbries which was either a chapel, a sacristy, or a dwelling.

PABBAY   NF 890870

The side walls and west gable with a rectangular doorway and a slit window survive of Teampull Mhoire, but little now remains of the smaller Teapull Beag to the west.

RODEL   A.M.   NG 047833

St Clement's is grandest medieval church in the Western Isles. It has small transepts not quite opposite each other. The chancel was probably newly completed in 1528 when the splendid tomb of Alasdair MacLeod of Dunvegan and Harris was built within it. It is set in a round arched recess within a gablet which has the Holy Trinity on the keystone. The voussoirs have pairs of Apostles alternating with angels. The effigy has its feet resting on what looks like a crocodile and there are many other carved panels. The effigy of William Macleod, d1552, lies west of the south transept arch. A more crudely carved effigy in the nave NW corner may be that of John MacLeod of Minginish, c1557. On the higher ground at the west end of the nave is a tower of five stages. Between the third and fourth stages is a rope-moulded string course rising in the centre of each face to frame a sculptured stone, the motifs being a bishop on the west, a bull on the north, two fishermen in a boat on the east, and a sheila-na-gig on the south. There are trefoil headed slit windows, those at the top having hood-moulds. The crenellated parapet is of the 1780s when the church was restored after being a ruin for two centuries. New nave windows were then provided. Harling was removed in 1913.

SOUTH UIST   NF 756365

Teampull Mor, the original medieval parish church of Howmore, with apart from a later SE adjunct only the east wall with two segmental-headed lancets with round rere-arches standing high, lies in the same graveyard as a chapel with a similar east window called Caibeal Dhiarmaid and a late mausoleum with an east doorway called Caibeal Nan Sagairt.

SWAINBOST   NB 508638

The east gable with a slit window and footings of the side walls remain of a medieval church of St Peter remodelled and enlarged c1790.

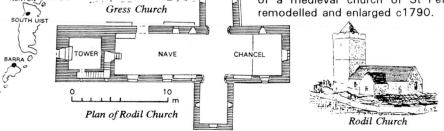

Gress Church

Plan of Rodil Church

TOWER   NAVE   CHANCEL

0 ___ 10 m

Rodil Church

EUROPIE
GALSTON
SWAINBOST
BRAGAR   GRESS
LEWIS
EYE
HARRIS
NORTHTON
PABBAY
RODEL
NORTH UIST
CHALUIM CHILLE
NUNTON   GRIMSAY
SOUTH UIST
BARRA

INDEX OF CHURCHES

Cathedrals and abbey churches mentioned in the introduction but not described in the gazetteers are marked *. Some churches on islands appear in the gazetteers under the headings in brackets after their names. On the maps unshaded dots are churches without individual gazetteer entries, and triangles are churches later than 1560 as they now stand.